Build Your Own Low-Budget Solar Power System

By
Steven Gregersen

Build Your Own Low-Budget Solar Power System

By
Steven Gregersen

Copyright held by the author.
All rights reserved.

This book may not be copied or reproduced in any form with the exception that small excerpts from the book may be used in reviews.

This book is dedicated to my mother,
the first and most important teacher, mentor, and inspiration in my life.

Table of Contents

Introduction (9)
Is a Low-Budget System Practical?

Chapter One (14)
Reduce Demand

Chapter Two (26)
Electrical Terms

Chapter Three (31)
Solar Power Basics

Chapter Four (50)
Inverters

Chapter Five (61)
Sizing the System

Chapter Six (74)
Generators

Chapter Seven (83)
Solar Power Kits

Chapter Eight (86)
Site and Installation Choices

Conclusion (93)

Introduction
Is a Low Budget System Practical?

I recently talked to a man who stated that while he likes the idea of off-grid living it was just too expensive for anyone except the rich. After some inquiries I learned that he had asked a professional to design a solar power system for his home. There are a lot of advantages to having a professional design and install a solar power system. But there are some drawbacks too. First, they tend toward over-sizing things. It's not just to make more money (although it does do that). It's mainly for customer satisfaction.

Few people with a professionally designed system will do the homework to understand what you can and cannot do when living on solar power. In order to cut down complaints from people who run low on power during cloudy spells they design a system that provides full power even on days when very little power is produced. That means you'll have extra solar panels, more batteries, a larger inverter and a bigger charge controller than you actually need. All because the customer wont take a couple of hours to attain a basic understanding of living off the grid.

Second; Professionals don't like getting a bad reputation from idiots! Let me give you a real life example. A neighbor (who has since moved away) called the company who installed their solar power system to complain that the batteries never reached full charge. She had been running her electricity for weeks of cloudy days on batteries that never even reached a fifty percent charge! To the uninitiated that means nothing. Those who understand the basics of solar power and battery banks have already cringed at what she's doing.

When you consistently run the batteries low on power you shorten the lifespan of the batteries. Their batteries (with an advertised ten year life expectancy), will probably last five years or less. Then they'll be griping to everyone who will listen how they were swindled by the solar power installer. Most reputable business owners will overbuild a system just to protect their reputation from ignorant customers like them.

Had she understood even the basics of solar power she'd have realized that when you have weeks of overcast days you need to reduce your electrical usage or supplement the solar panels with a generator. Unfortunately, the times when you need the most power are also the times when solar power generation is least effective. That needs to be taken into account when you design your system. (More about that later.)

Third; Professionals will have a lot of followup calls and visits to explain things their customers should already know. That takes time and costs them money. The professional installer who doesn't pad their bill a bit is going to lose money over the long haul.

Setting up a home solar power system doesn't have to be complicated or horrendously expensive. We've lived off grid on our twenty acre Montana homestead since 2003. There were two major incentives to live off the grid: first, it would have cost us $27,000.00 to get hooked up to grid power; second, we wanted to be as self-sufficient as possible. It was this self-sufficiency aspect that was most important to us. We just do not want to be dependent upon the power company... ever!

We began our life here with no electricity at all. We used kerosene lights for night time illumination in the living room of our cabin and the kids used solar powered "patio" lights for reading in bed.

Our first purchase was a 1400 watt gas-powered generator to run my power tools (needed for all the construction and remodeling work we were doing) but it was noisy and expensive to operate so was used only when absolutely necessary.

From that point we progressed to me taking an automotive battery to work where I charged it up in a back room. I'd take it home at the end of my shift and we'd use it, along with a 350-watt inverter, to run our laptop computer and power some low-watt fluorescent lights in the evening. When the battery ran down we repeated the process.

The next level was attained when we acquired a 64-watt solar panel through barter. An acquaintance wanted to trade the solar panel on their camp trailer for some repair work on their pickup. They had the parts but didn't have the tools or training required to install them. After a long afternoon of work we returned home with the solar panel and our adventure with solar officially began.

That first "system" was crude to say the least. It consisted of that single panel fastened to a wooden frame (angled toward the sun) that was fastened to the top of a large wooden spool discarded by the power company. We "turned" the spool during the day to keep the panel facing the sun.

At first we had no charge controller. We simply brought the battery out to the spool and hooked it to the panel using spring loaded clamps. It took all day long to recharge a battery but we were now "energy independent." It seemed like heaven to us!

From there we purchased another, 100-watt solar panel and a used charge controller. We then added more batteries, a 1000-watt Xantrex inverter and wired the whole thing together, including wiring the cabin with outlets. We purchased a fast charger from an automotive parts store so that we could charge the battery bank on cloudy days with the generator in a shorter amount of time.

When a neighbor upgraded his system we purchased their old 800-watt Trace inverter with a built in battery charger for about ten percent of what it would have cost new.

Our current system consists of seven, 130-watt panels (1120 watts total generating capacity), mounted on a pivoting steel frame so that we can turn the panels to attain the most direct sunlight; the same 800 watt Trace Inverter, a 1,000 watt Xantrex inverter, two PWM, Trace C-40 charge controllers, and eight, six-volt golf cart batteries.

This system allows us to operate an electric refrigerator, television, DVD/Blue Ray player, two notebook computers, and household lights. We still have the 4000-watt generator and we've added a 6000 watt generator to run my welder and air compressor.

We also have solar and wind power on our 33-foot motor home

that we use to head for a warmer climate to escape our long, Montana winters. It has 320 watts of solar power and a 400-watt wind generator, charging a battery bank of seven batteries. It runs everything on the motor home (including the electric refrigerator) except the air-conditioners.

We began our off-grid experience knowing almost nothing about solar power. As our system grew so did our knowledge.

It doesn't take a degree in electrical engineering to design and install a simple solar power system but it does take some homework. We've had a lot of inquiries from people desiring to set up their own off-grid power systems. Some have already tried and ended up with woefully inadequate systems lacking the power and balance needed for off-grid life. Others just don't want to do the homework required to; (a) design a balanced system; or, (b) understand what they can reasonably expect from a smaller system.

What we've learned is that, with careful planning and making some changes in your lifestyle it is possible to have your electrical needs met without investing a fortune in a home power system. Here's how!

Chapter One
Reduce Demand

In my experience the single most important element for low-budget, off-grid living is to reduce your need for electricity. That will save you more money than any other single step you can take. Ironically, if people would do this while on the grid they'd often reduce their electrical bill to the point that it wasn't economically viable to go off grid.

Going off the grid is a significant change from on-grid life. Instead of unlimited electricity you must now budget every watt you use. It's like going from life on a credit card to living on a strictly cash basis. With the credit card you can purchase whatever you want with no regard to how much you spend (until the end of the month at least!). When you live off-grid it's like a cash based budget. Spend it too fast and you run out of money! Then you can't spend anything until the end of the month. Once you've used up all the available power you don't get anymore until the batteries are recharged when the sun comes out. If you have weeks or months of cloudy days you will be without electricity for a long time.

When you think of electrical demand on a home power system visualize a fifty-gallon barrel of water. Water is running into the barrel at the rate of five-gallons-per-minute. The barrel also has a hose attached to the bottom in which the water is running out at the rate of ten-gallons-per-minute. It doesn't take a math wizard to see that the water is running out twice as fast as it's going in. Obviously you're going to run out of water. To avoid that you need to (a) reduce the rate the water flows out or (b) increase the rate the water flows in or (c) put in a larger reservoir or (d) some combination of the above.

To apply this to powering your home think of the water flowing in as your charging system (solar, wind or hydro power). Think of the barrel as the storage system which would be your batteries. The outflow is the amount of electricity you are using.

Obviously wind and solar energy outputs fluctuate according the amount of sunlight or wind you have available so you're going to need batteries to store the electricity they produce. The more batteries you have the more electricity you can store. The more or larger solar panels or wind generators you have the more power you can produce. The problem is that batteries, solar panels and wind generators are expensive. In addition, if you plan on running any 110 or 220 volt alternating current (AC) appliances you're going to need an inverter to convert the electricity stored in the batteries from direct current (DC) to alternating current (AC). Good inverters are (like everything else!) expensive, and the larger the inverter the more it's going to cost.

Step One: Cut Back on Your Electrical Needs

<u>Cutting back on your electrical needs is the most economical way to save money when setting up your home power system.</u>

By cutting back on your needs you can get by with a smaller inverter (which saves you money), fewer batteries (which saves you money) and fewer or smaller solar panels or wind generators (which also saves you money).

Before we get to this next section I want to tell you about a handy little gizmo called a "Kill-A-Watt" meter. It's a small, hand-held meter that you plug in the wiring between the power source and the appliance you're testing. It will tell you exactly how much power the appliance is using and is a much better way to figure your power draw than finding the manufacturer's data plate. They cost between $20.00 to $30.00 dollars and can be found at most hardware store. They'll make the next step easier and more precise.

Energy Use Spreadsheet

Appliances and Tools	Watts Run/Start	Essential Yes/No	Hours Used Daily	Home Power Friendly?	Altern- atives?	Total Daily Watts Used	Notes
Refrigerator	67-300 (Surge Watts)	Yes	24	No	Propane ?	1600	
Television	100	Yes	5	No	DVD Player?	500	
Lights (4 @ 60 W. each.)	240	Yes	8	No	LED	1920	
Vacuum Cleaner	1440 - 2160	Yes	4 wk.	No	Tile Floors?	820	
Automatic Washer	1150 - 1725	Yes	4 wk	No	Washtub ?	660	
Highest Surge Watts	2160				Total	5750	

16

Using the spreadsheet you should first take an inventory of everything on your property that uses electricity. Include all electrical appliances and tools from the big electricity hogs like the water heater and electric range, all the way down to the bulb used in the porch light.

Second, list the number of watts the item uses. (This will be found on the tool or appliance.) Some appliances use an amp rating instead of watts. Multiply the amps by the voltage to get the number of watts needed to run the appliance. For example: our vacuum cleaner uses twelve amps. 12 amps X 120 volts = 1440 watts. The reason you'll need to know how many watts are required is because solar panels, wind and gas generators and inverters are rated in watts rather than amps.

Some things may have two listings. One is the number of watts needed to start the tool or appliance. The other is the number of watts needed to run it once you get it going. Be sure to figure in the higher surge watt number too! Your inverter must be adequate for the highest figure.

Third, decide if this is an "essential" or "non-essential" item. This is entirely subjective. If mom or your teenage daughter (or son!) can't do without the hair dryer or curling iron then list it as essential. The same goes for dad. If he can't imagine life without his table saw (or curling iron?) then it too must be listed as essential.

Some things might be considered essential even if they are seldom used. We kept our waffle iron even though we use it only occasionally and need to start the generator to use it. (Although we later found one that works on the stove top and doesn't require electricity.) You decide what you want to keep.

Fourth, estimate how often and how long it's used. If it's daily then put daily (or weekly, etc.) For example, if you have a laptop computer that you use five hours, every day for work put 5h/5days in this column.

Fifth, is it "home power friendly"? For example: some televisions, VCR's, DVD players, etc. draw power even when the unit's power switch is turned off in order to maintain memory, run clocks, or energize "instant on" circuits. If you have appliances like these you'll want to be sure that (a) the batteries never go completely dead, or (b) you have an automatic back-up system such as a generator that will kick in if your batteries get low. There is a third option if you don't mind the clock flashing the wrong time or waiting a bit longer for the television to come on. You can put in a separate switch (we use multiple-outlet power strips) to completely shut off the power to the unit until you use it (and thus end the drain on your batteries).

The number of watts required to run the appliance may or may not be a red flag in this category. A microwave may draw a lot of power but only run for a few minutes whereas a toaster oven with the same watt rating may be in use thirty minutes or more. Obviously the toaster oven will use a lot more power in the long run. The same might be true of a circular saw when compared to a vacuum cleaner. They may both use the same amount of power per minute but the vacuum cleaner will be in use for longer time periods than the circular saw. (A quick note here: many microwaves do not like running off an inverter. It would be best to test it at the store before buying or, if that's not feasible, purchase one from an outlet that will let you return it if it won't work with an inverter.)

Sixth, are there practical, non-electric alternatives to the appliance? For example: a refrigerator or freezer may not use much electricity per hour but you'll need to have power to it twenty-four hours per day, seven days a week. That's no big deal if you're on the grid but when you're generating your own power it can be a problem. That doesn't mean you must go without a refrigerator. There are propane (and kerosene and gasoline) powered models that work just as well so under this column you'd write "propane."

There are also new energy-efficient electric refrigerators that use much less electricity than the old power hogs. We chose that option. Propane refrigerators are expensive. So much so that we could buy the extra solar panels and batteries to power our electric fridge and still have less invested than purchasing a propane unit. Plus we are not dependent upon purchasing propane.

Note: be cautious of "three way" or "two way" refrigerators like those used in recreational vehicles. Our "three way" (runs on propane, 12 volt DC, or 110 volt AC) refrigerator in our older motor home uses 240 watts-per-hour. For comparison, our home refrigerator is four times larger yet uses one-quarter as much power.

The same could be done for electric lights. There are also low watt (AKA "compact"), fluorescent and LED lights that work quite well and save a lot of electricity compared to incandescent bulbs.

An example from our household is the toaster. We like toast but due to the high electrical draw the toaster didn't make the move with us. However, we still have toast. We just make it on top of the wood stove. So under this column we wrote "use wood stove." If the wood stove isn't in use we make it in a skillet.

Seventh, in this column write in the total daily watts used by this appliance. Remember if it's a large draw item you only use once a week or so then take the number of watts used per hour times the number of hours used then divide by seven (days per week). Write the number in this column.

For example: The vacuum cleaner uses 1440 watts-per-hour and is used 4 hours per week. Four times 1440 equals 5,760 (total watts used during the week). Divide 5,760 with seven to get the daily watts used (823 watts).

Eighth, under this section write in your thoughts on the appliance in question. For example: you might want to write in "purchase propane refrigerator," or "purchase gas dryer." One thing to be aware of is that some gas appliances must have electricity to operate. We once owned a gas stove that had electrically powered oven controls. No electricity? No cake or cookies!

Important: Be sure you record the highest number of surge watts required by the appliances on your list. This will be important when choosing your inverter.

Step Two: Conserve Energy

This should be a basic part of everyone's routine whether on or off the grid. I can guarantee that if you go to someone's off-grid home you will not see lights left on in unoccupied rooms nor will you see a television left on with no one watching it. People tend to be wasteful when there's an abundance. Use only what you need. You don't need lots of overhead lighting if you're just lounging on the couch reading. Use an LED reading lamp drawing less than 3 watts.

If it doesn't need to be on, shut it off!

Other ways to conserve include using energy-efficient appliances whenever possible. Laptop and notebook computers need far less power than desk models and a fifteen-watt fluorescent bulb or 5-watt LED light puts out the same amount of illumination as a sixty watt incandescent bulb. Replace high draw items and appliances with energy efficient models.

Televisions are another big-draw item. That wall-sized television might impress the neighbors but is it worth the extra hundreds of dollars it will cost in solar panels, batteries and the larger inverter needed to power it?

Besides, most people watch too much television and spend too much time on the computer anyway. Do your mental and physical health a favor and improve your family life as well. Dump the big screen and super computer and go to the gym, go for a walk, go to the park, go fishing, take your wife out to dinner, or just curl up with a good book!

If you remodel your home put in some skylights or extra windows. Leave the blinds open during the day to let in natural light! You'll need less artificial light that way.

When you live off-grid you gain a new appreciation for the electrical power you use. Conservation becomes a way of life.

Step Three: Be Shrewd

Don't run the vacuum cleaner, iron, clothes washer, computer, etc at the same time. This saves you money in several ways.

First, your inverter must be able to handle the maximum load placed upon it.

If you start the vacuum cleaner <u>and</u> the washer at the same time *while using* the microwave (600 watts) you'll need a 5,000 watt or larger inverter. (Vacuum cleaner and washer require 2160 and 1725 surge watts to start while the microwave needs 600 watts to operate for a total of 4,485 watts.) If you run them one-at-a-time you can possibly get by with a 2500 watt inverter (although you may have to shut off the microwave to use the vacuum cleaner ... or just get a more energy-efficient vacuum cleaner!). Quality inverters are expensive and as the output of the inverter increases so does the price. By spreading out the demand you can use a smaller inverter. A smaller inverter is a cheaper inverter. A cheaper inverter means more money left in your pocket or extra money that can be used for other projects.

Second, spread the power usage out over the week.

Remember the water into the barrel <u>vs.</u> the water out of the barrel? If the bottom spigot is closed the fifty-gallon barrel will fill completely in ten minutes. Then if the spigot is opened all the way (ten gallons per minute) it will take ten minutes to empty it. (Remember, you are also putting in five gallons per minute while the spigot is open.) If you open it only three-fourths (7.5 gallons per minute) it will be twenty minutes before it runs dry. **<u>That's twice as much "run time" by reducing your draw by only twenty-five-percent.</u>** Your home power system works the same way.

When you produce more electricity than you are using, the batteries store it. The batteries allow you to use that excess power during times your system is not charging or when you're using power at a faster rate than the system is replenishing itself. Anytime you draw power out faster than you put it in you're going to run your batteries down. By spreading out the work you'll get by with fewer batteries and a smaller generating system.

So ... instead of doing the wash, vacuuming, and all the other housework in one day spread it out. Do the wash on Tuesday and Thursday and vacuum on Monday and Friday. Spend the other time reading, working in the garden, walking or doing something that doesn't require electricity.

Run the extra loads after your battery bank is charged and the sun is still going strong. For example, our battery bank is often fully recharged by noon on a sunny summer day. Once the battery bank is full the extra power produced by the panels is not being used. So I might use that time to run my brass tumbler to polish brass cartridge cases to prepare them for reloading. We may run one or more of our electric food dehydrators or we might use the electric grain grinder to restock our supply of flour or cornmeal. These are the times you have an excess of power so put them to use. Just don't use more than your panels can produce or you'll be discharging your battery bank and may not have enough power to last the night.

Step Four: Use a Generator for Big-Draw Items

We always counsel people to purchase a generator with their off-grid system. We were angry at one solar supplier who talked a friend into buying a larger inverter instead of a generator. We know him and he uses grid power for back-up to his solar system (plus he didn't sell generators so he made more money by selling a larger inverter). The friend was totally off grid so when she had a few days of cloudy weather they were out of electricity with no back-up plan! He also talked her into an 110 volt inverter when she needed one that had 220 volt capability. In the meantime she went without a generator for almost a year before she could afford one. That meant times with no power at all (meaning she also had times with no water from her well).

A 5,000-watt generator is much cheaper to purchase than a 5,000 watt inverter. When we fire up the generator we forget about step three. We may use the fast charger to charge batteries and use the electric grain mill (much faster than the hand mill!) to grind enough flour and corn to last a month or more. We might also run the vacuum cleaner, and/or use any high draw power tools like my shop equipment, cement mixer, etc.

However, don't rely upon the generator. Even diesel generators get expensive to run for long periods of time. Small, home use type generators have a short lifespan and use a lot of gasoline over time.

When you do purchase a generator get the best you can afford. A neighbor purchased a cheap 3500-watt unit. It wouldn't even run a small electric drill without tripping the breakers. The manufacturer would not stand behind it so he had to bypass the breakers to use it. Our 4,000-watt generator was the manufacturer's top-of-the-line model. It actually cost us more than the company's 5,500-watt unit but ours had features to promote longevity. Although I've had to do some minor repairs, it's still working well after thousands of hours of service. The added bonus is that it uses much less fuel than a larger unit.

You'll probably want one that produces at least 4,000 watts. We have three: a 3500-watt unit with our motor home and 4,000 and 6,000 watt units for auxiliary home power. (Our motor home also has a 400-watt wind generator and 320 watts of solar.)

We've pared our electrical usage down to the point that we wouldn't hook up to the grid if they ran the power lines under the front porch.

Chapter Two
Electrical Terms

In order to properly set up an off grid power system you must understand the ways electricity is measured. In this chapter we'll define some terms and look at formulas for converting volts to amps to watts.

A volt is a "unit of electric potential difference: the unit of electromotive force and electric potential difference equal to the difference between two points in a circuit carrying one ampere of current and dissipating one watt of power. Symbol V."

An ampere (or amp) is "SI unit of electric current: the basic unit of electric current in the SI system, equal to a current that produces a force of 2×10^{-7} newtons per meter between two parallel conductors in a vacuum. Symbol A."

A watt is a "unit of electrical power: the international SI unit of power equal to the power produced by a current of one ampere acting across a potential difference of one volt. Symbol W."

An ohm is a "unit of electrical resistance: the SI unit of electrical resistance, equal to the resistance between two points on a conductor when a potential difference of 1 volt produces a current of 1 ampere. Symbol Ω.

Note: All definitions above are from the Encarta ® World English Dictionary © & (P) 1998-2005 Microsoft Corporation. All rights reserved

Now that we know what we're talking about we'll continue … right? Wrong! Unless you're an electrical engineer the definitions above doesn't make a lot of sense so we'll try to understand them on layman's terms.

Now, please don't take these analogies to extremes. I've oversimplified some complex interactions in order to grasp some fundamental concepts.

Volts are a measurement of electrical force or pressure. The higher the number the greater the power or "pressure" of the electricity. It's like the pressure in a hose or water line. If you want to squirt water a long ways out of a hose you increase the pressure of the water. The same is true of voltage. High voltage power lines are used to "push" electricity thousands of miles. It's reduced when it gets to your home because it only needs to be "pushed" a short distance.

Amps are the "volume-of-flow-rate" of electricity. It's like the difference between a fire hose and your garden hose. If you run fifty pounds of pressure on each the amount of flow (or "amps") will be much higher on the fire hose simply because it can handle a larger volume of water.

Watts are a measurement of the total volume of electricity used in a specified time period of one hour. Kind of like "gallons-used-in-one-hour." The number of watts is a combination of pressure and volume (volts and amps). Using the fire hose example it's easy to see that you can fill a fifty gallon barrel with water faster using a fire hose than you can a garden hose. If you increase the pressure on each, the fire hose will always flow more water due to it's larger size. Now, theoretically, if you continually increase the pressure on the garden hose and keep the pressure on the fire hose low the garden hose will eventually flow as much water as the fire hose. However it will take a lot more pressure to do so because of "resistance" inherent in the smaller hose.

Resistance in electrical terms is called "ohms." It's the restraining force electricity must overcome to flow.

In the example above it takes a lot more power (or voltage) to flow a large amount of water through a garden hose simply because the small size of the garden hose creates a resistance to flow. Electricity is the same way. Even though we cannot see electricity with our eyes it still has physical properties just like water. If we want large amounts of electricity we must increase either the pressure or the volume or both.

If the resistance to the flow of electricity is too high we create heat. We use that principle in incandescent lights. The filament in the bulb is a small wire with high resistance. When the electricity flows through it the wire gets white hot and creates light.

That's also why a long extension cord with small wiring gets hot. We don't want this happening in extension cords though because bad things happen (like it catches stuff on fire!). Always use an extension cord that's adequate for the job at hand!

We're not going to compute resistance values but, as we'll see later, it is important to understand how resistance affects our power system.

These (volts, amps, watts) are all measurements of electrical energy and all three are present whenever electricity is being used. The problem we have is that devices that generate electricity and the devices that use electricity don't always list all three in the data plate.

Generators of all types (a solar panel is a generator that's powered by the sun) are rated in watts. Appliances are rated in volts and sometimes amps and sometimes watts. So we need some formulas for determining watts, amps, and volts in order to properly size our home-power system. As long as you know two of the numbers you can determine what the third number is.

Formulas to Determine Volts, Amps and Watts:

To determine the number of watts produced or used multiply the volts times the amps. V (volts) x A (amps) = W (watts).

Now people who do this for a living have different letters for their formulas using "E" for volts, "I" for amps and "P" for watts (and they have their reasons for doing so) but I'm trying to keep this as simple as possible so lets just stick to V, A, and W. Otherwise I'll get confused and I have enough problems with that already. So here are the formulas in the easiest format I can think of:

Volts are computed by dividing watts by amps. (W / A = V)
Amps are computed by dividing watts by volts. (W / V = A)
Watts are computed by multiplying volts and amps. (V x A = W)

We'll be using these equations throughout the rest of the book so you might want to mark this page or write them on a piece of paper and keep it close by.

Series vs. Parallel

You have different options for connecting the wiring of batteries and solar panels.

Parallel: Positive to positive and negative to negative doubles the amps but the voltage remains the same.

Batteries and solar panels have one positive and one negative post or wire. In a parallel circuit you connect the positive outlets together and negative outlets together. *Your voltage remains the same but the amperage increases.* For example, if you connect two twelve-volt batteries together, positive to positive and negative to negative your voltage remains at twelve volts but your amperage doubles.

Series: Positive to negative doubles the voltage but the amps remain the same.

When connecting the negative terminal to the positive terminal you double the voltage but the amperage stays the same. This is how you can use two, 6 volt batteries in a twelve volt system. Or you can connect two twelve volt or four six volt batteries to a 24-volt system.

It works the same way with solar panels. Connect the panels in parallel circuits and the voltage stays the same but the amperage increases. By connecting them in series you can increase the voltage but the amperage stays the same.

Chapter Three:
Solar Power Basics

Off-grid solar power systems are fairly simple and consist of solar panels, charge controller, batteries, inverter and wiring. If your power needs are miniscule you can get set up with just a solar panel and a battery.

It's important to note here that the system I'm describing is for off-grid applications only. Setting up a grid-tie system is more complicated so if that's your plan consult a professional.

I want to insert a section here on voltage options so that you can consider the positives and negatives of a 12 volt vs. 24 volt system as you read the rest of the chapter.

Voltage Options

In a low-budget, off-grid power system you'll most likely be working with either a 12 or 24 volt, battery/panel/inverter system. In deciding what's best for you remember that voltage is electrical pressure. A 24-volt system is more efficient (meaning less power is lost in transmission) than a 12-volt system.

Remember our illustration of a garden hose vs. a fire hose? The larger diameter fire hose can flow a larger volume of water because it has less resistance than the small diameter garden hose. If you increase the length of the hose you also increase resistance.

Try this experiment: Put a nozzle on a hose and turn the faucet up to full volume. See how far the hose will spray water. Now add another 50 feet of hose and try it again. You'll most likely see that the hose will not shoot water as far as before. Add another length of hose and try again. Now you'll see a further reduction in power at the nozzle. Now try garden hoses with different diameters. The small diameter hose will flow even less water.

The only way to get more water to flow through is to increase the pressure (voltage when talking about electricity). That's what happens when you go to a higher voltage in your solar power system. A 24 volt system has more power or pressure which increases the total amount of electricity (watts) flowing through the wiring.

This is why some manufacturers recommend a 24-volt system anytime the panels are 50 feet or more from the charge controllers and batteries.

Another reason in favor of a 24-volt system is that while your voltage doubles the amps remain the same. Charge controllers are rated in amps so you can run twice as many panels (producing twice as many watts of power) through your charge controller if you go to a 24-volt system instead of a 12-volt system. If you're opting for a large inverter (over 2400 watts) you'll probably have to go to a 24-volt system to handle the power demands.

The drawbacks to a 24-volt system? Everything will have to be purchased in pairs (or foursomes). It takes two 12-volt batteries connected in series to power a 24-volt system. If one battery goes bad you'll have to replace both batteries. It isn't a good practice to mix old and new batteries because the old batteries may draw the new batteries down. Your system will never be more efficient than it's weakest link. If you are running four, six-volt batteries to power a 24-volt system and one goes bad you should replace all four of them.

Likewise, if you buy 12-volt panels and wire them in series you'll have to buy them in pairs. It can sometimes be a challenge to come up with that much money. You'll need a 24-volt battery charger to run off your generator. And finally, if you switch to a 24-volt system after beginning with a 12-volt system you'll have to buy a new inverter (and possibly a charge controller) because they are not interchangeable between voltages.

Our system is 12-volts for several reasons. We began with one 12-volt panel and a used 12-volt, 800-watt Trace inverter. After that we added another panel, then three more, and then four more. To change to a 24-volt system we'd have to buy a new inverter ($1,000 and up), and at least one more panel. That's not going to happen anytime soon!

My recommendation is to stick with 12-volts unless your panels are over fifty feet from the battery bank and charge controller or you need an inverter rated over 2400 watts.

There is another option we'll discuss in the section on charge controllers. That's an MPPT (Maximum Power-Point Tracking) charge controller. These cost more than a PWM (Pulse Width Modulated) charge controller but they allow you more flexibility and allow the most efficient use of your panels.

Solar Panels

Solar panels are the primary component of most off-grid systems. Solar panels are nothing more than electrical generators powered by the sun. Like any other generator they're rated by their output in watts, volts and amps.

Shopping for solar panels can be confusing. When you talk to a salesman you're going to hear terms like "single-crystal silicon," "polycrystalline silicon" and "thin film." These are the three most common types of solar panel construction. Single-crystal silicon and polycrystalline silicon are the old standby's of solar modules. I could bore you with more details about how they're made and how they work but I won't. There's a lot of information on the internet going into more detail, so if you want to know more check out some of those websites. The most important information is that the original single-crystal silicon panels manufactured in the 1950's are still working today as are panels using polycrystalline technology from the 1980's. Their major strength is durability.

Thin film panels use various technologies to produce electricity. All tend to be less efficient and their durability factor is not yet known. However, manufacturing costs are lower than traditional methods and installation can be much more creative. Some are even transparent enough for use over windows and tough enough to be walked over. (Okay you have to be really careful walking on them but it can be done.) When applied to a roof they are not as susceptible to wind lift as traditional solar panels. This technology bears watching.

You'll hear a lot about efficiency and performance of different materials and manufacturing techniques. The differences are minimal. Generally, a more efficient panel has smaller external dimensions. In other words, a 100-watt panel with a higher efficiency rating isn't as large physically as a 100-watt panel that's less efficient. You'll also hear about some materials charging "sooner and later" than other materials. Again, the difference is slight. Compare prices and see if more "efficient" panels are worth the cost. Remember, a 100-watt panel still produces 100 watts of power no matter what it's made of.

Another issue regarding photo-voltaic (PV) panels is watt ratings. Watt ratings are the maximum power a solar panel can produce at it's maximum voltage. It's very important that you understand this.

Suppose you're considering a panel rated at 10 amps, 20 volts and 200 watts. However, your PWM (Pulse Width Modulated) charge controller will limit charging voltage to 15 volts (Note: voltage will vary according to battery type) to protect the batteries from being overcharged. To compute watts you multiply volts times amps. At it's maximum output of 20 volts and 10 amps the solar panel will produce 200 watts of power (20 volts times 10 amps equals 200 watts total output). However, the charge controller will limit voltage to 15 volts so now the output is 150 watts (15 volts times 10 amps equals 150 watts). You just lost twenty-five percent of the solar panel's maximum output when you installed it in your system.

Now don't get mad at the manufacturer or salesman. It's just the way things work. Solar panel manufacturers make many models for different needs. You'll need a solar panel with at least 15 volts to have enough power to adequately recharge your batteries in a 12-volt system. (Actually, due to other losses in the system you'll want a panel with a 17 volt or higher rating.) If you needed to produce 1,000 watts of power and thought your five (200-watt) panels would do the job you're going to be disappointed. In reality, the most they can produce at 15 volts is 750 watts. To ensure you can produce 1,000 watts you'll need two more panels. Just remember to do the math when you're sizing your system and purchasing panels.

Note: There is an exception to this. By going with an MPPT (Maximum Power-Point Tracking), charge controller you can take advantage of every volt/amp/watt your panels will produce. I'll cover that in more detail in the section on charge controllers.

Tracking the Sun

When a panel is "tracking the sun" it moves so that it faces the sun directly through it's entire arc across the sky. Solar panels produce most efficiently with direct sunlight. In the northern hemisphere solar panels are usually pointed south. They begin charging as soon as the sun rises but only hit peak output when the sun is shining more-or-less directly on them. Tracking devices increase the length of this peak output by turning the panels to keep them facing the sun. *In some cases you can gain forty-percent more output with a solar tracking system.* Depending upon price and local conditions it might be cheaper to increase your charging output with a sun tracker than to acquire more solar panels.

Plans are available over the internet for making your own tracking system or you can purchase one that's factory made. I've seen them offered as low as $700.00 dollars for a unit capable of holding six panels.

We have our panels set up on a pivoting mount. I change the angle twice per year depending upon the season then we turn the panels by hand during the day so that they continually face the sun. If we aren't going to be home during the day we lock the panels in the south facing position.

Batteries

Batteries store the excess power from your solar panels for use after the sun goes down or other times when your electrical loads are drawing out more than the panels are putting in.

Not all batteries are created equal. Automotive batteries designed to start your vehicle are constructed differently than deep-cycle batteries designed for sustained use. An automotive battery is there for only one purpose: that's to provide the power to operate the starter to start the motor of your vehicle. It needs one quick burst of energy for a few seconds. For this reason an automotive battery will have a larger number of thin plates in each cell. That way a larger part of the energy stored is instantly available.

As batteries charge and discharge the plates inside the battery actually change their chemical composition. This change occurs most rapidly at the surface. When a battery has a large number of plates it has more surface area exposed therefore it has more instantaneous power available. Since the outside of the plates discharge faster it leaves the inside with a residual charge. That kind of "seeps" it's way to the outer surface of the plates. It takes less time to "recharge" the surface of a thin plate than it does a thick plate. The downside is that while a thin plate recharges quickly it also stores less energy.

A deep cycle battery is designed to be charged up slowly and release energy slowly for an extended period of time. It will have fewer, but thicker plates in each cell in order to release it's energy at a lower rate but over a longer time period.

The most important number for an automotive battery is the CCA (Cold Cranking Amps). The most important numbers for a deep cycle battery are the Amp/Hour rating and the Reserve Capacity.

Since this is about solar power systems I'm not going into more details about automotive batteries. When it comes to batteries designed for off-grid power systems you'll have to choose between deep cycle batteries, golf cart batteries, sealed (or not) batteries, lead-acid batteries, Absorbed Glass Mat Sealed Lead Acid (AGM) batteries, Gelled Electrolyte Sealed Lead Acid (GEL) and a few others that aren't so well known. Each one has strengths and weaknesses. For the most part you'll get what you pay for so make your choice wisely.

The two most common types for the low-budget homesteader are the deep cycle batteries sold to boat and RV owners, and similar (but larger and more durable) golf cart batteries. Golf cart batteries are usually six volts so you'll need multiples of two for a 12-volt off-grid system and multiples of four if your system is 24-volts. The big complaint about regular deep cycle batteries is their short lifespan in off-grid applications. The big drawback to other types is the price. This is another area you'll need to do your own research before you make a purchase.

We've had about equal performance with both golf cart batteries and 12-volt deep cycle batteries. The 12-volt batteries make life simpler for us so we pretty much stick with them.

You'll hear different arguments about the lifespan of different types of batteries and while these may be good for comparative purposes, there's no way anyone can tell how long your batteries will last. The most important factors in battery life are how many charge/discharge cycles they go through, how deep these cycles are and how well you maintain them.

When a battery is discharged then recharged it's called one "cycle." The problem is that not all cycles are equal. The deeper your battery is discharged the more "wear" the battery sustains. Additionally, not bringing the battery up to full power before discharging it increases "wear" further. For this reason it's recommended that you have enough battery capacity to power your needs for five days without having to charge them. It may sound like a lot but if your storage capacity is too low you'll be discharging the batteries to a deeper level in each cycle which shortens battery life considerably.

Battery life is significantly extended if you discharge them no more than fifty percent of their capacity before recharging. Batteries are rated by how much energy is available from the full charge level down to the level where the battery is completely discharged. In order to ensure that the batteries are never discharged below fifty-percent some manufacturers recommend that you determine how much storage capacity you need then double that. For example: if you need 100 Ah of storage capacity it's recommended that you purchase the number or size of batteries required to achieve 200 Ah of storage capacity.

If you get in the habit of running your batteries in a continually discharged condition it will shorten their life. This often happens in the winter when daylight hours are short and nights are long. In these circumstances batteries may never reach full charge during the day so you're constantly using them in a partially discharged state.

Batteries function best in temperatures between 60 and 80 degrees Fahrenheit. Temperatures over one hundred degrees shorten battery life significantly. Colder temperatures require higher charging rates to bring the battery to full charge. If you store your batteries outside it's best to get a charge controller that compensates for battery temperature.

Batteries are rated by voltage and storage capacity.

Voltage is the number of volts the battery is rated at. This might be 2, 6, 12 or 24 depending upon battery type. Most batteries used for home power systems will be either six or twelve volt. Most charge controllers come in 12, 24, and 48 volt configuration. In order to get the correct voltage you put together different combinations. Two 6-volt batteries connected in series will equal 12 volts. Four six-volt batteries connected in series will get 24 volts as will two 12volt batteries. Unless you really know what you're doing I wouldn't recommend anything larger than a 24 volt system.

There are two ratings you'll want to take a look at. The first is the amp/hour (Ah) rating. The amp hour rating is the maximum sustained amperage that can be drawn from a fully charged battery over a specified time period (usually 20 hours) until the battery is dead. For example, our deep cycle batteries have a 125 amp/hour (Ah) rating. That means they can be discharged at a constant rate of 6.25 amps for twenty hours.

The second measurement is reserve capacity. Reserve capacity is the amount of minutes a battery *can maintain a useful voltage* under a constant 25 amp discharge. Our batteries have a 205 (minute) reserve capacity meaning that they can power a 25 amp load for 205 minutes without falling below 10.5 volts.

It's important to note that these are for comparison purposes only. Battery performance is impacted by it's age, number of discharge/recharge cycles, depths of discharge/charge, and temperature. Even the condition and size of the wiring and connectors affect the amount of power that's available. Wiring that's too small or connections that are loose (a fire hazard!) or corroded may significantly reduce storage capacity and output.

Remember the formula for converting volts and amps to watts? Multiply your volts by the amps to get the number of watts produced. A twelve-volt battery with a 125 Ah rating will produce 1500 watts over a twenty-hour time period. If you take the 1500 and divide it by 20 (total number of hours) you'll see that this battery, under ideal conditions, will power one 75-watt light bulb for 20 hours. In theory, it will power a laptop computer (50 watts) for approximately 30 hours. In reality, it won't last that long!

If you figure the watts of power available by the Ah (Amp hour) rating compared to the Reserve Capacity rating you'll get different numbers of watts available for use. The reason is that the rate of discharge impacts the amount of energy the battery can release. You'll get more power from a battery if you discharge it at a lower rate. The higher the discharge rate, the quicker the battery runs out of power.

The reason for this is because as a battery charges and discharges it changes the chemical composition of the plates themselves.

This change occurs first on the surface of the plates and continues inward until the plate's composition is equal all the way through. A fast rate of draw (as in the reserve capacity rating) soon discharges the outside of the plates. The center of the plate still has some charge left in it that hasn't "seeped" to the outer layer yet.

It's kind of like hydrating a sponge. If the sponge is completely dry and you sprinkle water on it, the outer surface becomes wet and soft while the inside or center still feels hard and dry. If you keep adding water the center will eventually become wet as well. This is the way the plates in your battery charge and discharge.

That's why you can run your battery down trying to start your vehicle then go inside, drink a cup of coffee, come back out and try again and the battery will once again power the starter. Of course it won't power it as long as the first time but what you've done is rest the battery so that the plates could equalize. Once again there's a surface charge to draw from.

Charge Controllers

The charge controller has only one purpose in life and that's to protect your battery from being overcharged. That being said, not all charge controllers are created equal. There are single stage and multiple stage charge controllers. A multistage controller has a few extra features that not only protect the battery(ies) but also enhance battery life and performance. Some of the small amperage, cheap charge controllers often used in RV's and most of the solar "kits" sold are not multistage units. They will only keep the batteries from overcharging. Battery life is sometimes significantly shorter with these units.

I'm going to classify Charge controllers into four categories: single-stage, multi-stage, PWM (Pulse Width Modulated), and MPPT (Maximum Power-Point Tracking). It's important to note that some of these features overlap in the better charge controllers.

A single stage controller does only one thing: Through some simple electronic technology, it regulates the maximum voltage from the panels to protect the batteries from overcharging. When the batteries reach a specific point the charge controller blocks the flow of electricity to keep it at safe (for the battery) levels. When voltage drops below a preset point it allows the panels to begin charging once more. These are often used in recreational vehicles. We have an old one in our U-haul conversion (motor home) that actually has a gauge instead of digital readouts.

As I've already mentioned, battery life may be significantly shorter and performance noticeably less with a single-stage controller when compared to a multistage controller.

In normal operating mode a multistage charge controller varies the voltage output of the solar panels according the charge level of your batteries. If your batteries are low the controller increases the allowed voltage to bring the batteries up to full charge quickly (bulk charge setting) then maintains that higher voltage (absorption phase) for a specific time period to ensure that the batteries are fully charged. Once that occurs it reduces the voltage (float or maintenance phase) to keep from overcharging the batteries.

They also put your batteries through an "equalization" (sometimes called "boiling") cycle every three to four weeks. In the equalization cycle the inverter increases the charge level significantly above normal for several hours in order to ensure that the battery is deeply charged.

Again, as a battery is discharged the outside of the plates discharge faster than the inside does. Because the charge level on the surface is less than at the center, the center of the plates slowly transfer power to the outer surface so that the voltage is equal throughout the plate.

When the battery is recharged the opposite occurs and the surface of the plates charge faster than the center. If the battery is discharged again before the inside of the plates are fully recharged you can end up with a situation where the inside is constantly undercharged and begins to deteriorate. The solution is to periodically overcharge the battery in order to "force" the electricity deeper into the battery's plates. This is called "equalization" because it's purpose is to equalize the charge level between the inside and surface of the battery's individual plates. When done properly it will extend the life of your batteries significantly.

Charge controllers are rated in amps and your solar panels are rated in watts. So once again you'll have to do a little math to chose the right one.

PWM (Pulse Width Modulated) charge controllers require that you wire your solar panels in parallel circuits. In other words, you may have six panels with a maximum output of 20 volts each hooked into a 12-volt system. That means the maximum voltage pushing the electricity to the charge controller is limited to 20 volts.

Your charge controller will list the maximum voltage they can handle. Do not exceed the manufacturer's listing.

This is an important point regarding charge controllers. A PWM or single stage charge controller functions like the voltage regulator in your vehicle. If the charging voltage from your panels exceeds the safe level for charging your battery the charge controller simply shuts out any additional power from your solar panels.

When shopping for solar panels you'll note that they all have different maximum voltage ratings. If the retailer does not list the "dollar-per-watt" price of the panel you should compute it yourself by dividing the number of watts the panel can produce with the price of the panel. What you'll normally find is that the price-per-watt goes down as the output of your panel goes up. This means that a 200-watt panel (producing 20 volts/10 amps) may sell for $200.00 (one-dollar per watt) whereas another panel putting out 64 watts (15.6 volts/4.1 amps) may sell for $130.00. That's over two-dollars per watt for the smaller panel! So what's the point of purchasing the smaller panel when you can pay half as much per watt for the larger panel and get more power?

To explain the answer I'm going to repeat what I said in the section on solar panels:

"Suppose you're considering a panel rated at 10 amps, 20 volts and 200 watts. However, your PWM (Pulse Width Modulated) charge controller will limit charging voltage to 15 volts (Note: voltage will vary according to battery type) to protect the batteries from being overcharged. To compute watts you multiply volts times amps. At it's maximum output of 20 volts and 10 amps the solar panel will produce 200 watts of power (20 volts times 10 amps equals 200 watts total output). However, the charge controller will limit voltage to 15 volts so now the output is 150 watts (15 volts times 10 amps equals 150 watts). You just lost twenty-five percent of the solar panel's maximum output when you installed it in your system."

"Now don't get mad at the manufacturer or salesman. It's just the way things work. Solar panel manufacturers make many models for different needs. You'll need a solar panel with at least 15 volts to have enough power to adequately recharge your batteries in a 12 volt system. (Actually, due to other losses in the system you'll want a panel with a 17 volt or higher rating.) If you needed to produce 1,000 watts of power and thought your

five (200 watt) panels would do the job you're going to be disappointed. In reality, the most they can produce at 15 volts is 750 watts. To ensure you can produce 1,000 watts you'll need two more panels. Just remember to do the math when you're sizing your system and purchasing panels."

Now, again doing the math, if you pay two hundred dollars for a 200 watt solar panel then reduce the useable voltage to 15 volts/150 watts, your per watt cost just went to 1.33 per watt. In this example you are still under the $2.00 per-watt price of the 64 watt panel and if you only want to produce the 150 watts of power (perhaps for a hunting cabin or RV) you still save money going with the larger panel even though you just lost 25 percent of it's available power.

But let's say you want a larger system. Perhaps one that will hit 1,000 watts of power. If you go with the five, 20-volt panels and a PWM controller you'll only have 750 watts of *available* power. If you want 1,000 watts of power you'll need two more panels (which will give you 1050 watts and cost an additional $400.00).

Depending upon the size of your charge controller you may also need two of those or maybe even three! Here's why! My two main charge controllers are Xantrex C-40's meaning they will handle up to 40 watts of *input* power. They can also be set to run on 12, 24 or 48 volt DC systems.

Notice that this is input power which means the power your solar panels produce. Each controller is adequate for four of the 200-watt panels. So with eight panels you'll need two controllers. With ten panels you'll need three charge controllers.

So for a 1,000 watt system you'll need three controllers at $150.00 each for a total of $450.00 and panels for a total of

$1600.00. Your cost for *only* the panels and controllers for a 1,000 watt PWM system will be $2,050.00.

If you increase the voltage to 24 volts by wiring your panels in series/parallel connections you could run twice as many panels per controller. (Remember, when you double the voltage in a series connection your amps remain the same.) You'll still need two of the C-40 controllers.

By going with a 24-volt system you can save $150.00.

(Remember, voltage is electrical pressure. I said earlier that some solar panel manufacturers recommend that you go to a 24-volt system if the solar panels are over fifty feet from your batteries and inverter because you need the extra voltage to overcome the resistance in the wiring. You could go to larger wire with 12-volt system but you may end up spending more for the wire than you did for the panels!)

Or ...

You can go with an **MPPT (Maximum Power-Point Tracking)** controller. By going with an MPPT (Maximum Power-Point Tracking), charge controller you can take advantage of every volt/amp/watt your panels will produce.

There are a couple of real advantages to MPPT controllers. First, with an MPPT controller you wire your solar panels in series circuits instead of parallel circuits as with the PWM controllers. The advantage here is that you can use smaller wiring from your panels to the controller.

Remember, voltage equals force or power. The advantage to going to a 24volt system is that you can use smaller wiring.

Imagine the savings when using a system producing 200 volts! So the first savings is in wire size.

The second savings is in the increase in the amount of useable power being generated. You'll need a minimum voltage of at least 13.5 volts to begin charging a low battery. In a parallel connection, *each panel* must be producing 13.5 volts to begin charging the battery. Solar panels only reach maximum production under direct or nearly direct sunlight. If you can't track the sun you may not get enough power out of your panels to charge your batteries until mid-morning and you may only get enough direct sunlight for full charging capabilities for about five hours each day. If your panels are only generating 10 volts each you can't charge your batteries.

Because you hook your panels up in series with an MPPT controller you'll gain about 30 percent more charge from your solar panels. The reason is that the amount of power produced by each panel is cumulative. In other words, if you have eight panels and each one is producing 10 volts the charge controller has 80 volts to work with. With eight panels each panel needs to generate only two volts (16 volts total) to begin charging the batteries on a 12 volt system. They're doing that almost as soon as the sun comes up so you may gain several hours of extra charge time during the day just by switching to an MPPT controller.

Cloudy days will also greatly reduce your power from a solar charging system but with an MPPT controller you'll still get some power to your battery bank even on days when the sun doesn't shine.

Going back to our previous illustration using five, 200-watt panels lets crunch some numbers.

MPPT controllers figure their maximum voltage limit using the panels' Open Circuit Voltage. These are higher than the "Maximum Power" rating on the panel. We'll assume that the Open Circuit Voltage of our 20 volt/200-watt panels is 25 volts. With five panels wired in series that totals 125 volts of Open Circuit Voltage. Our five panels have a total watt rating of 1,000 watts and total Open Circuit Voltage of 125 volts. For that combination we'll need an Outback Flex Max 80 or it's equivalent. These sell for about $520.00 at this time. So we have $1,000.00 in panels and $520.00 for a charge controller. That totals $1520.00 for 1,000 watts of solar power on a twelve volt battery bank.

That compares to $2050.00 if you used PWM controllers to give you the same maximum output. (A savings of $530.00!)

And that's not all. You've also increased the total amount of electricity per day. Remember, you'll get an increase of about thirty-percent per day with the MPPT controller. So instead of five hours at the maximum charge rate of 1,000 watts-per-hour (5,000 watts total daily production) you'll be getting 6,500 watts of daily electrical output. And this at an initial savings of $530.00 over using a PWM system.

It always pays to do the math when setting up a solar power system. Prices vary considerably but if you purchase panels for under one-dollar per-watt and go with an MPPT controller you'll almost always save money.

Our solar power system was built in stages so we have the PWM controllers. When I build the next one it will be with an MPPT controller. Do the math!

Chapter Four:
Inverters

The charge controller takes the power from the solar panels and charges the batteries with it. The inverter changes the twelve volts of DC (direct current) from the batteries to 120 or 240 volts of alternating current (AC). (If your system is 24 or 48 volts the inverter also converts that to 120 or 240 volts AC.)

If you're not familiar with AC/DC current, AC (alternating current) is what you get through your power lines. It's electricity that changes direction from positive to negative. The number of times it changes direction every second is called a cycle or, more commonly "hertz." In the U. S. our electric grid functions at 60 hertz (the electricity changes polarity 60 times each second). It's sometimes different in other countries.

DC, or direct current is electricity that travels in one direction only. Your vehicle operates on DC while your household appliances operate on AC. You can purchase DC appliances but generally it makes more sense to just buy an inverter and use the things you've always used.

That being said, it's a good idea to have some 12 volt receptacles around. We use aftermarket gizmos similar to the cigarette lighter socket (now known as the "accessory power supply port") in your vehicle. You can purchase these at discount and auto parts stores. Some nicer looking units can be purchased from recreational vehicle supply retailers. You'll pay more but they look much better inside your home.

Most cell phones, portable computers, cameras, etc. can be charged through these 12 volt power ports. It's a little more efficient than converting 12-volt battery bank power to 120-volt AC power then back to the five to twelve volts DC needed to recharge small batteries in your phone, tablet or whatever.

Inverters have outputs of 120 and/or 240 volts. The 240-volt will give you a little more versatility. 240 volts are better if you're going to run your well pump off your inverter.

Sine Waves

When looking at inverters the first thing you'll probably hear about are "sine waves."
Remember that in a 60 hertz (Hz) system the direction of flow changes 60 times every second. The best way to visualize this is to draw a horizontal line then put a "plus" above the line and a "minus" below the line. Now draw a bunch of "waves" through the line so the peaks and valleys are an equal distance above and below the lines. If you could see electricity as it enters your house from the power line it would look like this as it changed direction from positive to negative. These are called "sine waves."

AC Current Flow

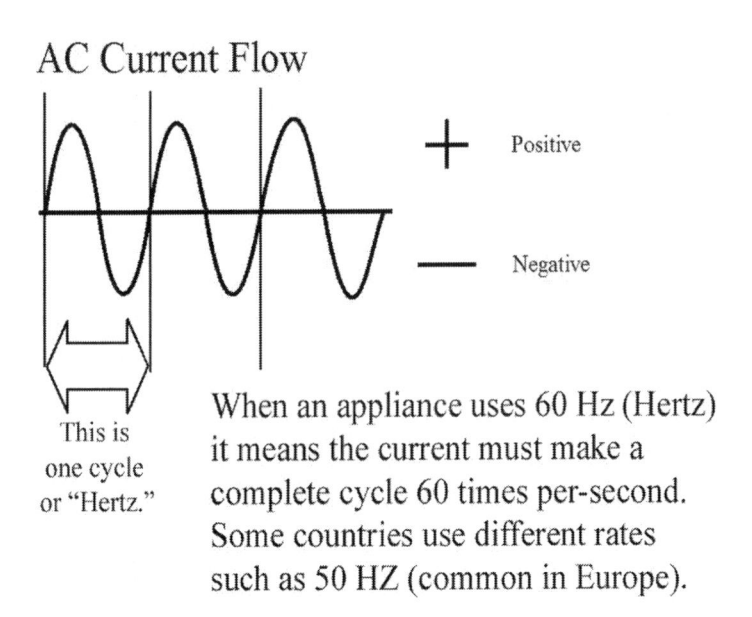

+ Positive
— Negative

This is one cycle or "Hertz."

When an appliance uses 60 Hz (Hertz) it means the current must make a complete cycle 60 times per-second. Some countries use different rates such as 50 HZ (common in Europe).

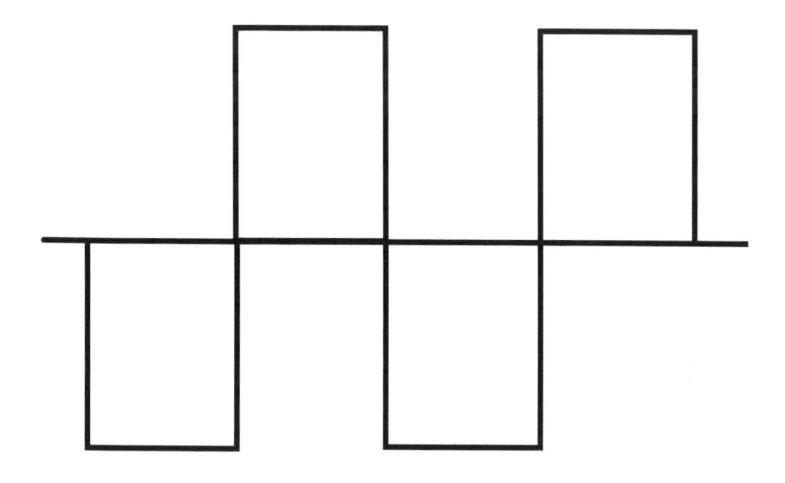

This is a straight
"sine wave" inverter.
You don't see
these much anymore.

Positive

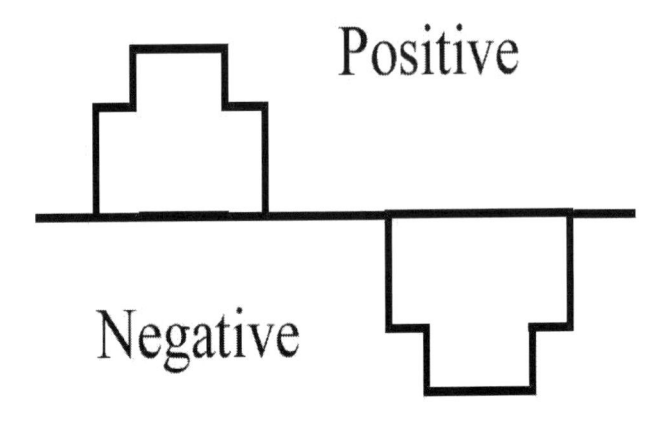

Negative

This is a "modified" sine wave. Note that the changes are not so abrupt or extreme as a straight sine wave.

Positive

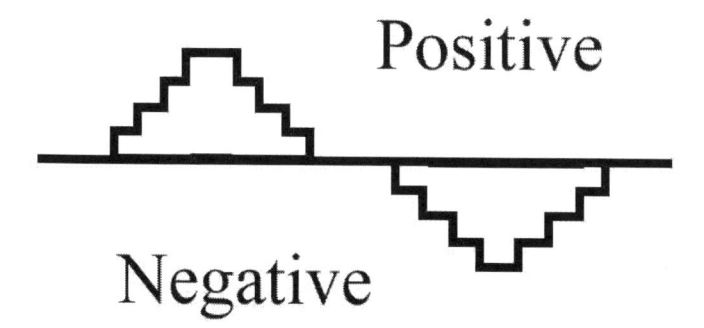

Negative

This is a more sophisticated example of a modified sine wave inverter. Note that the "steps" are smaller and more numerous giving a pattern much closer to a true sine wave.

The problem with inverters is that they are digital. They can only turn electricity on or off. To represent this you draw the horizontal line again but instead of drawing "waves" intersecting the line you make a vertical line above the horizontal line then a short line parallel to the horizontal line then another vertical line that goes an equal distance to the negative side, another horizontal line then another vertical line up ... repeating this process over and over again. This is what a basic, square wave, inverter would do to change DC current into AC current.

The problem is that many electrical appliances cannot function with such abrupt changes of direction. So inverter manufacturers have what they call modified sine wave inverters. Instead of switching the current from positive to negative so abruptly they do it in stages. Instead of having lines going straight up and down with horizontal "ledges" between them, the inverter does it more like a staircase. The smaller the steps on the staircase, the more "pure" the sine wave. Thus the difference between a pure sine wave inverter and a modified sine wave inverter is the size of the "steps." A pure sine wave is like riding on the waves with a gentle rise and fall with the swells. A square wave is more like riding on top of a piston in your vehicle's engine. You go straight up, hang for a split second then go straight down again, hang for a split second then get slammed upward again (and again and a gain and again and ...). Now, which would be the gentlest on your body? It's the same with electrical gadgetry.

Most modern inverters are a modified sine wave. They've broken these cycles into progressive steps to more closely mimic a true sine wave. The problem is that you have no way of knowing how sophisticated the programming is on a modified sine wave inverter. The best guideline is that you get what you pay for. Now that doesn't mean that cheaper inverters won't work for you.

We've used several brands of "cheap" inverters with good results in everything except our microwave oven. The main part of our off-grid cabin is powered by a $79.95, 1,000 watt inverter from Costco. Our boys spent countless hours playing X-Box and computer games using cheap inverters. My advice is to give them a try if you can't afford a higher quality inverter. Just do so knowing what to expect regarding duty cycles, surge watts, and life expectancy.

It's important to note that even pure sine wave inverters use a modified sine wave. The difference is that they use oscillators and more sophisticated programming so that the sine wave generated is almost indistinguishable from those supplied through grid power. The main selling point to pure sine wave inverters is that they lengthen the life expectancy of your electrical appliances. But even that is minimal compared to a good modified sine wave inverter.

Duty Cycles or Continuous Watt Ratings

Inverters have what are called "duty cycles." Duty cycles are the amount of time a device can work at a specific percentage of maximum output before it needs to rest. It's the difference between running or sprinting. A person running a marathon goes at a slower pace than a person running a hundred yard sprint. Inverters are the same. If you put a huge load on them it won't be long before they overheat and must take a break. However, if you use a smaller load they'll continue working for hours without stopping.

Our Trace inverter is rated at 800 watts output for 30 minutes before it overheats and shuts down. If the load is 600 watts it can go for 60 minutes but if the load is 575 watts it can go forever without needing a break.

This is one of the first places you can tell a difference between a high or low quality inverter. Low quality inverters have a much lower 100 percent duty cycle than better quality (more expensive) inverters.

Surge Watts

Many appliances need an extra boost to get started. Since these surges are short lived, most inverters and generators have enough power available (called "surge watts") for a few seconds to get things started. As soon as the appliance or tool is running it's power needs diminish substantially. Here's another place you can tell the difference between a low- vs. high-quality inverter. Our 800-watt Trace inverter's surge watt capacity is 2400 watts while our cheaper, 1,000-watt inverter's surge rating is ... 1,000 watts.

A note about wiring and inverter placement: Generally the largest wiring you'll need is the wiring from your battery bank to the inverter. For this reason it's a good practice to have the inverter near the battery bank but not in the same compartment or too close to the batteries. The batteries put out corrosive gas and if your inverter is too close you'll soon be replacing it.

Do not skimp on the wiring to the inverter! Wire for a 2400-watt or larger inverter may cost as much as $5.00 per foot. This is one of those situations where there are no safe shortcuts. If the wire is too small it will overheat and performance will suffer. If your safety devices (fuses or circuit breakers) are too large the wire can get hot enough to catch nearby items on fire. The inverter instructions should have recommended wire sizes. If it doesn't, contact the manufacturer. Follow their recommendations to the letter!

A word to the wise on surge ratings and duty cycles. I can't say that every cheap inverter is over rated but I can say that the four different brands of cheap inverters we've used have all performed significantly under their manufacturer's assertions. So, should you avoid cheap inverters? Not necessarily. Just be aware that a cheap inverter will probably not do all that the manufacturer's claim. Again, this is my experience in using them. You may have different results.

Voltage

You'll have to decide on whether you want an inverter that has only 110-volt AC output power or an inverter with 110- and 220-volt options. I recommend that if your inverter is rated at 2,400 watts or more you go with an 110/220-volt inverter. Many appliances run more efficiently on 220 volts. Well pumps are a prime example. You can get 110-volt deep-well pumps but it's easier to find them in 220-volts and they work better and last longer than the lower voltage pumps.

This is another area you'll have to decide for yourself!

Battery Charging

Inverters can be purchased with or without built-in battery chargers. There is conflicting information from different manufacturers on the good/bad points of the built in-battery charger. Naturally, the people who don't build chargers into their inverters say that an external charger is the best way to go while the people who do build chargers into their inverters say that their way is best.

My preferences go to the inverters with built-in chargers. Primarily because they are tailored to the specific needs of off-grid power. Your solar panels' charge controllers have different charge levels depending upon the stage of charge your batteries are in. When the batteries are low they increase the charge voltage to around 14.9 volts to bring the batteries to full charge quickly then maintain that higher voltage (called the "absorption" phase) for a time period to ensure that the battery's plates get a full charge. After that they reduce the voltage to approximately 13.0 to 13.5 volts for what's called the "float" or "maintenance" setting to keep from overcharging the battery. The charger built into the inverter changes voltage to accommodate each stage. Automotive type battery chargers are limited to a compromise setting of approximately 13.8 volts maximum.

If you have a 24-volt or larger system an automotive type charger probably won't be an option for you. You'll have to use an inverter with a built in battery charger.

That being said, we used an automotive charger for a couple of years with no apparent ill effects on our batteries.

Inverters with built-in chargers usually have transfer switches so that when you start your generator or plug them into the grid (with grid-tie systems) they automatically transfer the load from your batteries to the outside power source and also activate the charger to recharge your battery bank. In some cases the "switch" is done so quickly that your computer won't even know it happened.

For example: When we fire up the generator and plug it into the inverter the inverter flips an internal switch that sends the full power generated by the inverter into our cabin's electrical wiring. Now instead of being limited to the normal 800 watts we have through the inverter we have 4,000 watts available directly from the generator.

Chapter Five:
Sizing the System

Okay, we've looked at reducing your power demands and using your power wisely. We've looked at solar panels, and batteries and inverters and charge controllers so what's next? Now we put it all together.

I'm repeating myself somewhat here but bear with me. This is perhaps the most important section of the book!

Remember in Chapter One we looked at the Electrical Appliance Worksheet? Now it's time to put it to work. Begin going across the rows and adding things up. Suppose in line one, you have a laptop computer that takes fifty watts of power and you use it five hours a day for five days a week. That gives a daily total of 250 watt/hours per day.

A small, energy-efficient, refrigerator draws about 200 watts of power. A refrigerator only runs about a third of the time on average so the per-hour watt rating is approximately 67 watts. It's on 24 hours a day though so the daily total will be 1608 watts (rounded off to 1600).

We could continue with examples but I think you understand what we're doing here so go on down the list estimating your daily electrical consumption. If an item (such as a vacuum cleaner) is used only sporadically like four hours a week don't worry about it yet. What we're looking for is a starting point to estimate how large your battery bank and solar generating capabilities need to be. Once you've finished the daily tally add them all up. For example we'll assume 250 for the computer, 1600 for the fridge, another 500 for the television, and maybe 1920 for lights (you should swap the incandescent lights for LED's). The total per-day usage is 4270 watts.

Now look at the occasional-use items. The vacuum cleaner used four-hours-per-week at 1440 watts-per-hour totals 5760 watts per week. The washer at four hours per-week using 1150 watts-per-hour totals 4600 watts per week. Go on down the list and total these up then take that number and divide it by seven. This is the average use per day. It's important to include these items otherwise your system will not be large enough.

So we have 4270 watts per day plus an average of 1480 watts per day for occasional use items which means that our total daily, energy use estimate is 5750 watts. We'll round it off at 5800 watts. **Write that number down!**

Resistance

Remember earlier when I said we'd look at resistance later? It's now "later." Resistance in any form is the force that impedes motion. In electrical jargon it's called "ohms." Think of it as the difference between bicycling on the level with no wind to bicycling uphill against the wind. There is no such thing as a perpetual motion machine because resistance makes that impossible.

For example: if you draw 100 watts of power from a battery it takes 125 watts of power to recharge it to it's previous level because of internal resistance in the battery. When electricity flows through the wiring from your panel to the batteries some of the energy is used up to overcome the resistance in the wiring.

If you used 5800 watts of electricity you will have to generate approximately thirty-percent more (1740 watts) than that to compensate for the resistance in the system. That means you'll have to be able to generate 7600 (rounded up from 7540) watts to replace the energy you've used.

If you're using solar panels they only charge when the sun is up and they only charge at their maximum under direct sunlight. There are charts available online showing how many hours of direct sunlight you'll receive in the part of the country you live in. What you'll want to know is how many hours of direct sunlight you can expect in the shortest day of the year. Why? Because if you size your system for the most hours of sunlight you can get on the longest days you won't be able to generate enough electricity on the short days. If you size the system to be adequate on the short days you'll (almost) always have adequate power all year long. If you don't want to look up the charts use five hours as a default figure. This means that your solar panels need to generate 7600 watts in five hours or 1600 watts per hour(round up from 1520). You'll need enough panels in the right combination to meet that number.

So far we have:
7600 watts daily use.
5000 watts in solar panel output.

Your charge controller must be adequate for the solar panel's maximum output. You can use two or more charge controllers if necessary. (That's what we did when we added four more panels to our system.) Another thing you can do is go to a 24 volt system rather than a 12 volt system. With a 12 volt system you'll need one charge controller rated at about 75 amps or two rated at approximately 40 amps. Or you can go with an MPPT controller that will handle the output of your system.

Now we have:
7600 watts daily use.
1000 watts in solar panels.
85 amp charge controller (or an equal combination of smaller controllers)

Batteries should be able to power all your needs for a minimum of three days with five days being preferred. The reason for this is so that you won't be constantly running your batteries down completely or running them extensively in a discharged condition. The more batteries you have in your battery bank the easier it is on the batteries and the longer their life expectancy will be. There is an exception though! I've seen homes with huge battery banks and inadequate solar generation.

Citing one example: They could last a week (seven days) with no input from their solar panels but they didn't have enough solar panels to get the batteries recharged in a reasonable length of time. They would run their batteries in a low charge condition for weeks at a time. They had a generator to power a charge controller with a built in 80 amp charger and it was not adequate to completely recharge their battery bank after running the generator for ten hours straight!

The problem with a battery bank that's too large is recharging it once you've run it down. People tend to pay too little attention to the details. They'll look at the readout on the voltmeter and think that they're only a little bit low on charge levels. What they don't realize is how much charging the battery bank will need to return to full charge.

Let's go back to our 50 gallon barrel analogy: if you close the spigot on the barrel it will take ten minutes to fill the barrel if the water is flowing in at five gallons per-minute. Remember, the barrel represents your battery bank. Now, what if instead of having a fifty-gallon barrel you have a 50,000 gallon swimming pool! At the rate of five-gallons-per-minute it would take 10,000 minutes (167 hours/7 days) to refill it. And that's only if you are not drawing anything out during that time.

This is what happens if your battery bank is too large for the amount of solar power generation you have available.

It's best to have a balanced system.

So to size your battery bank with ample power for three days, take 7600 multiplied by three for a total of 22,800 watts. Batteries are rated in Ah (amp hours) so we divide 22,800 watts by 12 volts to get 1900 Ah for three days. If your batteries are rated at 125 Ah each you'll need 15 batteries to get you through three days.

For five days storage capacity you'll need 38,000 watts divided by 12 volts for 3167 Ah storage capacity. Again, using the 125 AH number you'll need 25 batteries.

Now, batteries are rated under ideal conditions. By the time you add the inverter, wiring, connections and temperature variations you're going to loose 25 to 30 percent of your power to that bad guy known as "resistance" (and some other factors) so increase your battery estimates by 25 percent. That means you'll need 19 batteries for three days reserve or 31 batteries for five days reserve.

Now we have:
7600 watts daily use.
1000 watts in solar panels.
85 amp charge controller (or an equal combination of smaller controllers).
19 batteries (three days), or 31 batteries (five days).

The inverter must be large enough to handle the highest load expected of it including surge watts. When it comes to inverters the price will vary significantly depending upon which inverter you purchase. It is especially true that you get what you pay for when purchasing an inverter. Lower-priced units are lower priced for a lot of reasons. That doesn't mean they won't be functional. Just be aware of their limitations.

In our case here, we've got the vacuum cleaner and washing machine listed as the highest draw items. Assuming that neither are used at the same time we can figure the run watts at 1440 and the surge watts at 2160 watts. The fridge may be on at any time as will the computer. So on a day when the computer is on (50 watts), the television (100 watts), the vacuum cleaner (1440 watts), and the fridge (200 run watts) you'll be drawing 1790 watts of power. You might have a few lights on as well which with LED lighting may only be another 30 watts, but it all adds up! So we have a continual load at 1820 watts (50+100+1440+200+30=1820 watts). Plus, you'll have the surge loads when the vacuum is turned on initially. This may add another 720 watts to the total for a few second's time so your inverter must be capable of at least 1820 watts continual (100 percent duty cycle) load and 2540 watts surge load. I'm going to use the approximate cost of a 2000-watt heavy duty inverter with a built-in battery charger. It will run approximately $1200.00 to $1800.00.

Now we have:
7600 watts daily use.
1000 watts in solar panels.
85 amp charge controller (or an equal combination of smaller controllers).
19 batteries (three days), or 31 batteries (five days).
2000-watt inverter

The estimated cost of these items will be approximately:
$1000.00 - 1000 watts in solar panels.
   520.00 - MPPT charge controller
  1900.00 - 19 batteries - three days, ...
  3100.00 - 31 (12 v) batteries - five days.($100.00 ea.)
  <u>1200.00 -</u> 1 inverter
$4620.00 Total cost for a 3 day battery bank, or ...
$5820.00 Total cost for a 5 day battery bank

These prices do not include wiring and hardware for mounting panels. Also, this is a very minimal system for the majority of people.

There's another thing you should note as well. The daily use of the appliances we've listed is greater than the daily output of your solar panels.

Remember, even with the MPPT controller the expected output will only average around 6500 watts per day, However, the daily use is estimated at 7600 watts. You're already starting with a system that is too small ... maybe! Plus, your solar panels won't be able to charge up your batteries even on a good day because you'll be drawing out more than you're putting back in. Your solar charging system must put out enough power to not only recharge the batteries but also put out enough power to cover your electrical use during the day.

<u>Read On: Do Not Get Discouraged!</u>

I can show you how to cut those figures by fifty-percent just by cutting your electrical usage even more and buying a generator. It's not that difficult.

Look back at the energy use spreadsheet. If you go with a propane fridge you can deduct 1600 watts. If you go with a notebook computer you can reduce the 250 watts to approximately 125 watts. Use LED lights to cut that column down from 1920 watts to 200 watts or less. We purchased a small, portable DVD player for our grandson to use. It uses about 30 watts-per-hour and will play for several hours on the built in battery once it's charged up. On overcast or cloudy days he watches his movies on it instead of the television. Our television was purchased because it only uses 53 watts at maximum power (volume). That was half of what our previous television used.

On three items, by purchasing with off-grid life in mind, we cut our daily electrical usage from 4,270 watts to 575 watts. That's a reduction of 3,695 watts per day. Note that on our theoretical list we also went to a propane refrigerator. Small, 10 cubic-foot propane refrigerators start around $1400.00 which is why we don't have one. (In our own case we used the money saved to purchase more solar panels then bought an energy-efficient electric refrigerator for under $300.00. We spent a thousand dollars upgrading our solar power system and we'll never have to buy propane, and we still came out ahead.)

So even if we stay with the fridge on the chart and make the other changes our daily watt usage will only be 2,175. That's over a fifty-percent reduction on the upper portion (not counting the vacuum and washer). If you include the washer and vacuum the daily total is still only 3,655 watts.

Now use a generator for the high draw, seldom used appliances. There will be more information about choosing a generator in a later chapter but for now I just want to point out that you can easily find at this time (September 2014) a 4,000-watt generator for under $500.00. We currently own two Champion Generators (3500-watt and 6,000-watt) and one Generac 4,000-watt model.

Now, let's look again at how much it will cost to set up your solar power system.

First, we will stay with the electric fridge so our daily watt use will be 2,175. We'll round that up to 2200 watts then add in 30 percent for system losses which means our daily power generation need is now 2860 watts (2200 + % = 2860). That's 4740 watts less than our previous figure!

Let's go with 750 watts in solar panels. With five hours of direct sunlight we'll generate 3750 watts and by using an MPPT controller we can add another thirty percent to that which brings the daily total to 4875 watts. Our daily use is 2,175 watts so we have a surplus of 2700 watts. That surplus goes to recharging the battery bank.

Our inverter needs to have enough output to run our appliances along with any expected power surges. In our estimate the only inductive motor that will cause a power surge is the refrigerator. The general rule for figuring power surges is to add fifty-percent to the watts needed to "run" the appliance once it starts working. In this case we'll need an inverter with at least a three-hundred watt surge rating. If everything is working at the same time our draw will be: 25 for notebook computer, plus 200 for the fridge, plus 50 for the television, plus 25 for the lights which equals 300 watts. Add in another 100 watts to accommodate the power surge when the fridge kicks in and y*ou'll need an inverter that puts out 300 watts at a 100 percent duty cycle* with a 400-watt surge rating.

My advice would be to go with a minimum rating of 600-watt inverter/charger. An example of what's available is the Magnum MM6 12AE for about $500.00. It has a 950-watt (five minute) surge rating and 600 watts continuous. It also has a built-in 30 amp charger to recharge the battery bank while it's on generator or grid power. There are similar units available from other manufacturers.

The battery bank can also be smaller. With a peak daily draw of 2200 watts we'll need a battery bank that can handle that plus another 25 to 30 percent for internal losses. That puts it at (again) 2860 watts. A three day battery bank will need to store 8600 watts (rounded up from 8580) and a five day battery bank will need to store 14,300 watts. Batteries are rated in amp/hours (AH) so divide the watts by 12 (volts) to arrive at the suitable storage capacity in AH. For three days that's 717 AH (8600/12= 716.66666). For five days the amount is 1192 AH (14,300/12=1191.66666). At 125 AH per battery we'll need 6 batteries (717/125=5.736) or for five days we'll need 10 batteries (1192/125=9.536).

We'll also need a generator for the high-draw appliances. What you'll want to do here is run the generator on the days you wash clothes and run the vacuum. If you can do both at the same time you'll only need to run the generator for four hours per week. If you wait until the battery bank is low (as in a period of overcast weather) you can recharge the battery bank at the same time. Most 4,000 watt generators are easy on fuel so four hours per week doesn't break the bank.

This is the method we use and it works well.

So, look at the numbers now:

$750.00 in solar panels
$500.00 for MPPT charge controller
$500.00 for the Inverter/charger
$600.00 batteries for three days or
$1,000.00 in batteries for five days.

We'll also need to add in a generator for $500.00

That's:

$2850.00 with a three day battery bank and generator, or ...
$3250.00 with a five day battery bank and generator.

That's $1770.00 less than the previous amount for three days and $2570.00 less than the previous five day estimate.

Obviously your needs will vary from those I've listed. We know of no one else that is as frugal on electrical use as we are. The primary goal here is to help you see what a huge difference a few minor changes can make in the overall cost of going off the grid.

If you are like me, doing the math is tedious and extremely boring but it can literally save you thousands of dollars in set-up costs.

In our case it would have cost us over $27,000.00 to get hooked up to the grid. That's <u>Twenty-seven-thousand-dollars</u>! And then we'd have been stuck with monthly utility payments and the periodic power outages.

We opted to live without electricity instead. When the opportunity arose to get a solar panel in trade for a few hours of labor we took it. We began with nothing and slowly built up our off-grid system in stages. Instead of having a household full of electrical appliances and "gearing down," we began with nothing and added to it as our solar power generation increased. It didn't feel as if we were losing ground by going solar. It felt like we were becoming fabulously rich!

So instead of forking over five-grand we began with a small, 65-watt solar panel and worked our way up from there in stages.

The key is to use this information to design your own system that fits your needs and budget.

You may not be able to afford a full-house solar power system and you may not even want one! We get a lot of inquiries from people who just want solar as an emergency back-up or they want to power parts of their home by solar.

These are great ideas and with the information you've read so far you can do that. It's the same process to set up a system for emergency power for a fridge or freezer as it is to power part of your home or to power your entire home.

You need to know first your power requirements, then you put determine how many solar panels you need, what size of charge controller and inverter will work best and how many batteries are required to back up the system.

If you've done all that and set up your system and still have problems here are some guidelines to go with:

1. If, by sunset on a sunny day, your battery bank is not fully charged, you need more generating capacity (more solar panels) or less electrical usage.

2. If you run out of power during the night (before your panels begin charging) then you need more storage capacity (more batteries) or less electrical power usage during the evening and night.

In the concluding chapters I will address what you need to look for when purchasing a generator and I'll go over some of the pros and cons of solar power "kits" as sold through some of the major retailers. In the last chapter (8) I will discuss site and installation concerns.

So. on to the next chapter!

Chapter Six:
Generators

I've seen a few people try to set up an off-grid home without a generator and they've usually regretted it. Even with a first class solar power system there will be times when (a) you have extended periods of overcast or stormy conditions or, (b) the system needs to be shut down for maintenance. Therefore it's wise to make a good choice when purchasing a generator.

If you go the opposite extreme and are planning on running a generator all day long think about this: a generator that will survive continuous duty is very expensive to purchase and run. If you thought your previous electric bills were pricey wait until you purchase gasoline, diesel or propane to run a generator 4,380 hours a year (12 hours per day for 365 days a year). We've known people who've tried it. Not only is it expensive but the noise will not be appreciated by neighbors who moved out in the woods seeking peace and quiet. In addition, if your goal was to conserve our natural resources, running a generator for hours at a stretch will definitely defeat that purpose.

Even if you just use the generator to charge your battery bank it's going to be expensive. It's also harder on batteries because the battery bank must drop to low levels before the generator kicks in. As we stated in the sections on batteries, the depths to which a battery is drawn down can be harder on the battery than the number of cycles. In most generator/battery banks systems I've seen the batteries are drawn down substantially more than a solar power system. Mainly because the solar energy recharges the battery bank every day even when it was only partially discharged.

So while I believe off-grid homes should have a generator for back-up and/or high draw items, I don't think a generator is good as a stand-alone system.

Generators come in all sizes and prices ranging from $100.00 for new 1,000 watt portable units to thousands of dollars for large generators mounted permanently with automatic transfer switches. With these you don't even have to be home when the power goes out. Everything is automatic from turning the unit on when the grid goes down to turning it back off when things are back to normal. But, before you rush out to purchase a standby generator there are some things to consider.

Size

Begin by reviewing your power demands. Any generator you purchase needs to be large enough to run essential appliances or tools.

Generators, like inverters, have two watt ratings. The lower number is "running watts." This is what the generator can be expected to produce as long as it's running. The higher number will be the "surge watts." This is what the generator can produce for a short length of time (a few seconds) without overheating or damaging the unit. Be absolutely sure that your generator can handle the highest surge load you have listed.

In my experience it's better to have a generator that's larger than you think you'll need rather than one that's barely adequate. You may need extra power to overcome resistance in any extension cords you're using. Also, older appliances or tools may use more power than they did in their prime. Likewise, as a generator ages it may not be as powerful as it was in its youth. Other factors such as altitude, temperature, humidity or fuel quality may keep your unit from reaching it's maximum potential. I'd recommend a generator rated twenty-five percent or more above your estimated power needs.

Why not just buy a big generator and not worry about watt ratings? Big generators produce more power but use more fuel. (A serious consideration if you're going to run it more than a few hours!) Larger generators usually cost more than similarly equipped smaller units. Finally, smaller (portable) generators are easier to transport.

Outlets

If you're using a portable unit you'll need to know if it has an adequate number of outlets with amp ratings that will meet your needs. Of course you can use power strips and other devices to connect multiple cords to a single outlet but be sure these devices are rated to handle the current those loads will demand from them. Generally the smaller the watt rating the fewer outlets you'll have. Outlets should be convenient to use where they won't be subjected to fuel spills or oil leakage and where you won't get burned by the exhaust.

Noise

Noise is rated in decibels. Anything over ninety decibels (db.) can damage hearing. Some typical sound levels include: residential area without traffic (40 db.), normal conversation (60 db.), normal street noise/average radio (70 db.), truck without a muffler (90 db.), lawn mower (100db.), trains (110 db.), jet aircraft/artillery fire (140 db.).

If you plan on using a generator at a secluded retreat noise is definitely a concern. The only thing that will advertise to the world that you have power and they don't faster than a loud generator is a brightly lit house at night. Even with temporary power outages in the suburbs you're going to have neighbors calling to use your generator.

Stealth reasons aside there are other reasons you should be concerned about noise. It's difficult to concentrate on tasks when being bombarded with noise, and in already stressful situations it's even worse. Plus hearing can be permanently impaired by high noise levels.

There are generators that address the noise problem but they normally cost twice as much as their similarly rated (output), but noisier cousins. If you want one of the quiet units be sure the salesman knows and be prepared to spend more money!

Fuel

Most portable generators use gasoline. Other fuel options include propane, natural gas, and diesel fuel. Each has good and bad points. Whatever fuel you need be sure to have an adequate supply on hand for emergency use.

Gasoline

Gasoline is easily obtained now and can be stored in large or small containers. It's the most common fuel choice on portable units. If you store your gasoline for long time periods be sure to use a fuel stabilizer.

It's also wise to read the manufacturer's instructions for long-term storage of your generator. Many advise that you drain all gasoline from the tank and carburetor if the unit will not be used for extended time periods.

Propane

Propane has a long shelf life and can be easily stored in small or large tanks. It's not as convenient to purchase as gasoline but is still easy to get. If you use a bulk tank you'll have to have a propane company fill the tank. (But you won't need to buy any for a while either!) Most propane generators are permanently mounted, "whole house" units.

Natural Gas

Natural gas is clean burning and as long as the gas lines are functioning you have an unlimited supply of fuel piped to your home. It's usually available in times of crisis. Earthquakes are the most dangerous threat to natural gas lines. These units are permanently mounted.

Note: Some natural gas-powered generators require higher gas pressure than that used by your home's supplier. If this is the case find out if your NG supplier can install a meter with the higher line pressure. If they do, you'll need a separate gas regulator to reduce the pressure for the other appliances that use

NG for fuel.

Diesel Fuel

Diesel fuel is easily obtained and the least flammable (safer to store) of the four. Bulk delivery is available if you have a large enough tank (talk to the nearest supplier). Diesel generators are usually large and may be either portable (usually mounted on a trailer) or stationary. You can use red-dye fuel for off road use and avoid some of the taxes levied on automotive fuels.

A note on fuel consumption: most generator manufacturer's list a fuel consumption rate at fifty-percent load. Just remember that the higher the load the more fuel it will consume and plan your fuel reserves accordingly.

Portable or Stationary

Stationary generators are usually mounted on cement pads. Permanent installations are easy to use and can often be wired so that you can start and run them from the house. Also, most stationary units have bulk tanks so you don't have to refuel every few hours. The disadvantages include expense (they're usually large and pricey), and you can't take it with you if you need to bug out.

Portable units are, well, portable. You can take them with you if you leave or take them where the power is needed. If the weather's extremely cold you can bring them in the house to warm them up prior to trying to start them. (Something to think about when it's twenty-five-below outside!) Portable units are also cheaper. Some disadvantages include small fuel tanks that will need frequent refueling and extension cords must be run from the generator to the appliance(s) or your inverter/charger.

Make sure extension cords are properly sized to carry the electric load, as overloaded cords can overheat and cause fires.

Small units (under fifty pounds) can be moved by carrying. Mid-size generators usually have wheel kits available to roll them to new locations by hand. Large generators can be mounted on trailers to pull behind a vehicle.

Any generator used in an enclosed area may cause a build-up of carbon monoxide or other harmful gases. Set them up outdoors in a well-ventilated area away from living quarters.

Liquid or Air Cooled

Liquid cooled engines run at a more consistent temperature for longer engine life and better performance. These are usually large, stationary (sometimes trailer mounted), generators designed to run non-stop for days, weeks or months at a time. You'll usually see these as back-up units at hospitals or public buildings and as part of the equipment of emergency response units.

Almost all small, portable (not trailer mounted) gasoline generators are air cooled. They function quite well for use by the homeowner as long as they're used in open areas with good ventilation (the only safe place to use one anyway!).

Design Features

Now that you have the basics down it's time to look at some optional features that you may or may not consider necessary.

*Overhead Valve engines start easier and last longer than side valve engines.

*Cast iron cylinder sleeves in aluminum engines reduce cylinder wear and extend engine life.

*Low-oil shutdown switches shut down the engine if the oil level drops below a safe operating level. Don't rely on them. I've seen them fail. Keep a close watch on oil levels. *Always* check the engine oil level before starting the unit.

*Electric start enables easy starting without having to pull a starter rope. If you want this be sure your unit comes with a battery (Some don't!). It's especially helpful in cold climates where generators might need a little extra spin or longer cranking before they'll start. Two of ours have electric starters.

*Idle control switches let the engine throttle down when no load is present. They save fuel and wear on the generator and cut down on noise levels while idling. They are especially helpful when using a generator for construction projects where you might run a saw every few minutes and don't want to have to keep restarting the generator each time. By idling down between times you'll save time and use only slightly more gasoline during the day.

*Hour meters keep track of how long the motor's been running. (Very helpful for maintenance purposes.) Even with an hour meter you'll need to keep a log of run time between maintenance sessions. The hour meter just makes it easier!

*External/replaceable oil filters extend engine life.

*Full power switches allow you to switch off the 240 volt output to get more power to your 120 volt outlets. This is especially useful when powering air compressors and water pumps with a minimally sized generator.

*Brushless alternators require less maintenance and produce power that's more suitable for sensitive electronic equipment.

There are other options available (mainly on high-end, permanently mounted units). Most of these add to the cost and aren't necessary unless you're powering a hospital or office with a lot of electronic equipment. Use your own judgment when talking to a salesman.

Even if you don't live off-grid a generator is a good thing to have on hand. In our "town days" we used ours almost every time a severe storm rolled through. A neighbor or friend always seemed to need it to run their refrigerator or sump pump when the power went out.

Chapter Seven:
Solar Power "Kits"

We constantly field questions regarding solar power "kits" like those sold through outlets like Harbor Freight Tools, Costco, Cabelas, Northern Tool & Equipment, etc. I don't want to cut them down too bad but their main selling point is convenience. They've already done the math and put together the pieces into one convenient package but let's look at what you're getting for your money.

One example is a major retailer who offers a 300-watt solar panel kit for $899.00. It comes with two solar panels, a 30 amp, digital charge controller, a 300 watt inverter, wiring and mounting hardware. I did a quick internet search and I'll show you what you can get for $899.00 by purchasing your own components. I can get two, 255-watt, 31 volt panels for $482.00 ($241.00 each); a 30 amp MPPT charge controller for $280.00; a thousand watt inverter for $79.00; and the wire and mounting hardware for another $30.00. That's $871 for a system that puts out 510 watts (compared to 300), with a charge controller of much higher quality and efficiency (30 percent higher output from the panels which boosts their *daily* output from 2550 watts to 3315 watts), and a 1,000-watt inverter (700 watts more than their 300 watt inverter), and wiring and mounting hardware for $28.00 less than the pre-packaged unit. With both systems you'll still need to acquire some batteries to charge and store the electricity.

Savings can be had on even the smaller systems like this 45-watt system sold by many retailers: It includes three 15 watt panels, charge controller, wiring, and a PVC frame to prop the panels up. You need to supply the inverter and battery. List price is $299.00 but it can be found on sale for around $200.00.

To build your own you can purchase one 55-watt panel for $160.00, and a 7-amp charge controller for $19.95. The total is $180.00. Mounting hardware can be purchased at any hardware store for a couple of dollars. If it was mine I'd just wire it up and lean it against something so that it faced the sun. You can find a 12-volt power jack (outlet) at any hardware or auto-parts store.

In both cases you can find a 350-watt inverter for around $25.00 to $35.00. New deep-cycle batteries run from $60.00 to $120.00.

I can do the same thing with virtually any solar power kit on the market. You can too! A caution: most of these kits are low-powered. They'll do for a light or two and maybe a laptop computer or a portable DVD player. Don't plan on running your refrigerator or freezer when the power goes out.

The advantage of the kit is convenience. Someone else has purchased the individual parts and packaged them up for you.

You'll also see solar "power stations" advertised for sometimes thousands of dollars! They're often trailer mounted units claiming a discharge rate of 5,000 watt (more or less) solar power stations.

Read the list of materials closely. I've seen these things with just 500 watts of solar panels, a couple of deep cycle batteries, and a large inverter. The batteries would quickly run down if you attempted to draw 5,000 watts for an extended time period.

Think about what you've learned. 500-watt panels will put 2,500 watts of energy into a battery on a typical day. A deep-cycle battery will typically store 1500 watts of power. Two batteries would store 3,000 watts of power. It will take all day plus a couple of extra hours to recharge the battery bank. The inverter at full capacity will drain the batteries in about an hour and twelve minutes. Now you're out of power until the sun comes out to recharge the battery bank. You're much better off to just purchase a generator.

Chapter Eight:
Site and Installation Choices

Where you put your solar panels is as important as the number of them you have. I cannot stress enough that solar panels need as much direct sunlight as possible.

Many falsely believe that if a solar panel is getting sunlight on half the surface area it is still functioning at fifty-percent of it's rated capacity. Nothing could be farther from the truth!

I conducted an experiment once in which I covered two out of 72 grid sections (total number in the solar panel) resulting in a thirty-five-percent loss in power production by that solar panel.

I next covered fifteen grid sections (approximately twenty-percent of the surface area) which resulted in a fifty-percent drop in power produced by the panel.

At fifty-percent shade the panel's output was reduced to 1/2 amp.

The reason this happens is because the solar panel tries to equalize the voltage between the cells. If half of the cells are not producing electricity the power produced by those cells that are making electricity goes to "charge" the unproductive cells.

The same thing is happening to every solar panel that is connected together. If one panel is in the shade, the other panels will try to charge that one before they'll charge your batteries.

It's like having a series of barrels all linked together with pipe at the bottom. The last barrel has an outlet at the top and that's where you'll get the water from. But, you won't get anything out of the upper discharge outlet until all of the barrels are full. Every drop of water poured into *any* of the barrels will be used to fill *all* of the barrels.

The most important aspect of site selection is having as much direct sunlight as possible for the most hours possible during the day.

That's the main reason you can often increase power 40 percent by using a sun tracking system for your solar panels. It keeps them pointed directly at the sun.

Be aware that temperature makes a difference as well. Unlike most things, solar panels actually function at their highest efficiency in cold weather. Heat has the opposite effect so the cooler you can keep your panels the better they'll produce electricity.

I prefer mounting panels on a tower rather than a roof for this reason among others. (The second reason is for tracking the sun. The third is a distinct aversion to making more holes in my roof!)

If you mount your panels to a roof, wall or other structure be sure to leave adequate room for air flow around the panels to help keep them cool. Most manufacturers have minimum recommendations. Follow them.

Solar panels have holes in the back side of the frame. You can use these holes as mounting locations to bolt your panels to whatever frame you have designed. You can also purchase clamps to clamp the solar panels to mounting frames. The clamps are more convenient for roof mounts or other types of mounts where access to the underside of the panels is difficult.

I've seen panels bolted to steel frames, aluminum frames, plastic pipe, metal pipe, and wood frames. Our first panel was bolted to a wood frame that was nailed on top of an old utility company wire spool. We set up another set of panels temporarily by bolting them to wooden cross bars nailed to an old outdoor swing frame. I even saw one person wire theirs to a wood frame. I've seen campers (people, not vehicles) who just put their panels on the ground, propping them up with rocks or boards to face the sun more directly. Others have mounted "legs" to theirs to prop them up facing the sun.

The first time we used a solar panel with our U-Haul truck converted to a motor home, we just propped the panel against a small utility trailer next to the motor home.

Another acquaintance used a solar panel kit and set it and the frame on top of his motor home. A gust of wind blew it off one night. While it isn't recommended to throw your solar panels off a roof this one escaped harm without even a scratch on it's tempered glass surface.

These things are pretty tough!

In short, there is no "right" or "wrong" way to mount solar panels as long as they are placed where they'll get the most direct sunlight and be anchored in such a way that the wind can't blow them into the next county. It also helps to have them at a level where you can periodically clean off any dirt, mud, grime, leaves, etc.

In our Montana home debris isn't a problem. We get enough rain to wash off what little dust accumulates and they are far enough from trees that leaves are not a problem (we also have mostly pine trees that don't shed their needles). We do, however, need to brush the snow from them frequently during the winter.

Batteries should be kept where they'll avoid temperature extremes and have good ventilation. Batteries give off hydrogen gas (which is explosive) when charging. They also give off corrosive gasses so keep them separate from electronics like the inverter and charge controller.

If your batteries are subject to extreme temperatures get battery temperature sensors for your charge controller. That way the charge controller can manipulate charging voltages to compensate for low or high temperatures.

Both charge controllers and inverters will have directions and diagrams with suggested ways of wiring your system depending upon what you want to achieve. Follow them. They will vary according to the way the inverter and controller are installed in the system, charging voltage, battery bank voltage, etc.

 Also follow the recommended wire size charts supplied. Do not use wire sizes (called wire "gauge") that are too small. System performance will suffer and you may also burn your home down. Small wires overheat when you ask too much of them.
Overheating wire may or may not trip a breaker or blow a fuse. If it doesn't blow the fuse it might start a fire. (Remember what I

said about an incandescent light?)

Typically for a small, 12 volt, stand-alone system (not grid tie) you'll have your solar panels wired (in series or parallel according to the system voltage and the type of charge controller you have) into your charge controller.

The output wiring from the charge controller will go directly to the battery bank. The battery bank will be wired in parallel or series depending upon it's voltage and the voltage of the batteries. (The simplest system will be 12 volts using 12 volt batteries. In that case you just wire the batteries in parallel circuits.)

The wires from the battery bank will go to the inverter. These will be heavy gauge (thick!) cables that can handle a lot of amps! It helps to have the inverter as close as possible to the battery bank. (But not so close that corrosion will be a problem.)

From the inverter your wiring will go to the entry panel of your home or cabin. After that point it is wired and fused like any on-grid structure.

It's normally best to have one single ground rod for the entire system. You can use a regular ground rod purchased for that purpose from any hardware or electrical supply outlet. Bury it as deep and straight into the ground as possible. Eight feet is considered minimum in moist soil. However, you may need more grounding. Local conditions determine the best depth so ask a local electrical contractor or the county building inspector to learn requirements for your area.

Your charge controller instructions will give you options for the grounding system. Choose the one that's best for your installation.

I like to have fuses or breakers on the inverter and charge controller sides of the battery bank, one between the battery bank and solar panels and breakers for each panel (It's nice to be able to isolate individual panels for maintenance or repair purposes).

For low voltage, direct current fuses or breakers go to your auto parts store or an outlet specializing in solar and off-grid power. Do not use AC type breakers for DC applications unless the manufacturer specifically condones it.

Once your wiring is at the entry panel for your home use regular, breakers or fuses designed for 120/240 AC systems.

Again, it can sound complicated but it isn't. It's mostly just tedious! Pay attention to the details.

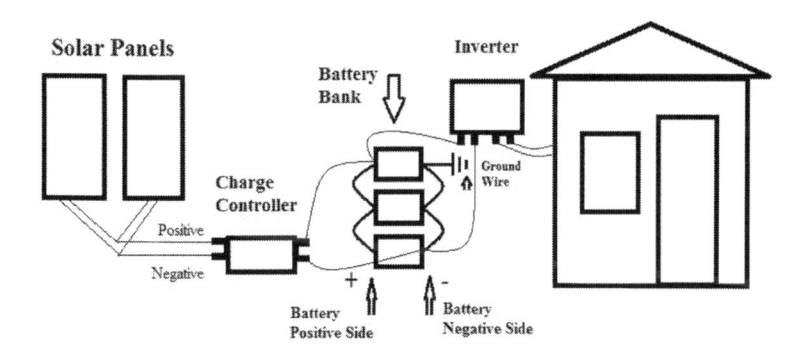

This would be a typical wiring diagram for a small, 12 volt stand-alone system as described in this book. You should have the negative side of the battery bank grounded to an approved grounding system. The ground terminal or the case of your charge controller(s) and inverter should be grounded through the household electrical ground. The metal frames of the solar panels should each be grounded to the metal framework of the tower or other mounts being used and the tower should be grounded in an approved manner. If the frame the panels are attached to is not a conductor of electricity then the panels should be grounded to a common ground at or near their location.

Ground the generator (if you have one) according to the manufacturer's recommendations. Most people do not ground portable generators even though it might prevent electrical shock if something malfunctions.

There should be circuit breakers or fuses on the positive wires between the panel array and the charge controller; between the charge controller and battery bank; and between the battery bank and inverter. Note: the capacity of the circuit breaker or fuse will vary according to the output amperage of each unit. Follow the manufacturer's recommendations.

Keep all wiring as short as possible. Locate your panels, charge controller, battery bank and inverter as close to the residence or structure as is practical.

Be sure to check with local building authorities and your insurance company. In some places additional steps must be taken to comply with local regulations and zoning.

There are a lot of different opinions regarding ground circuits for photovoltaic systems but even though electrical engineers may disagree on what is necessary or not necessary and even disagree whether some legally required ground circuits might actually harm the system under certain conditions, it will still be the law that taps you on the shoulder if you don't do things their way. Do your best to comply with all applicable building codes and laws.

Conclusion

Life off the grid can be either great or a total disaster. The biggest problem we've seen with people new to off-grid living is that they try to live the same way off the grid as they did while hooked up to grid power. Unless you've invested a pile of money into your system you just can't do that. In reality, it would be foolish to try.

Every time you reduce your need for electricity you reduce the price of your off grid power system. (Often by thousands of dollars!) That should be very plain by now.

But you'll also want to be more aware of conditions around you. You'll begin to notice cloudy or overcast days and automatically reduce the power you use to accommodate outside conditions. One off-grid family we know was asked what they do when they have several days of cloudy weather. They simply responded that they use less electricity.

The opposite is also true. On sunny days you can splurge! Once the battery bank is charged everything for the rest of the day is a surplus and we take advantage of it without a twinge of guilt! Want to run the big computer with it's larger screen? Go for it! Want to run the electric food dehydrator? Do it!

Our neighbor uses an electric lawn mower to mow their grass. It's a great idea. Our summer days are long with lots of power generation. Why not do something good for your wallet and the environment? (We use push-type reel mowers.)

We've adapted so well over the years that we seldom use our generator except for my shop equipment. And even then we put less than 50 hours per year on the generators. We often go weeks without ever starting a generator.

Living off-grid calls for a huge change in the lifestyle of most Americans. But the changes are good if you'll just embrace them. Your power is now just outside your door. Even though our on-grid friends and neighbors endure power outages throughout the year, the only time we've been out of power was one night when a lightning strike took out our phone and inverter. We just switched all power to the other inverter then the next day installed a new inverter to replace the blown one (we keep a spare on hand). That's the only time we've been without power since our first solar panel was hooked up.

One third of a successful off-grid life is energy conservation.

Another third is attitude. If you believe you're sacrificing your life and happiness to live off-grid you're going to be miserable. Get off the martyr complex and enjoy life. Read a book! Play cards! Take a hike or take up some hobbies that don't require electricity! Take pride in your energy conservation and the changes you made to adapt. You are the envy of a lot of people who just don't possess the fortitude you've displayed. It won't be long until rather than envy those on the grid, you'll start to look askance on their abysmal waste of energy.

The last third is understanding how your off-grid system functions. Why is that important? Because you 'll know what to expect! It will cut down your frustration level immensely. You'll see the need for variable power usage and recognize the limitations of your system.

We know one couple whose wife called the firm that sold and installed their off-grid system every day to complain that she had run out of power. Her expectations from the start were way too high. It wasn't a real problem during the long days of summer but when the short days and long nights of winter arrived she whined endlessly. Finally she accepted the limitations and learned to live with it. If she had understood the basics in the first place she'd have avoided a lot of frustration.

By reading this book you've taken an important first step in acquiring a basic understanding of how a solar power system operates.

Even if you never move off the grid you have a better grasp on how much power you need to run your household. If you just use that knowledge you could probably cut your utility bills in half.

As for us, the next system we set up will be done differently. Had I known then what I know now we'd have saved a thousand or more dollars on our present system.

Hopefully that money savings will carry on to you as well.

If you enjoyed this book you'll want to check out some of the other books written by this author. Go to the Web Page for Amazon Books and type in a search for the author's name. You'll bring up titles like:

*Creating the Low-Budget Homestead
*The Gun Guide for People Who Know Nothing About Firearms
*The Beginner's Guide to Reloading Ammunition: With Space and Money Saving Tips for Apartment Dwellers and Those on a Budget
*The Greenhorn's Guide to Chainsaws and Firewood Cutting

You can find my blog by going to: http://livinglifeoff-grid.blogspot.com/. This chronicles our life as off-grid, (almost) self-sufficient homesteaders on our 20 acre homestead in northwestern, Montana.

My wife also has numerous books published. Type in a search on the Amazon Books site for Susan Gregersen.

Some of her best seller's include:

*Poverty Prepping: How to Stock Up for Tomorrow When You Can't Afford to Eat Today
*Food Storage: Preserving Fruits, Nuts and Seeds
*Food Storage: Preserving Meat, Dairy and Eggs

She has many more listings in both fiction and non-fiction books. Her blog can be viewed at: http://povertyprepping.blogspot.com/

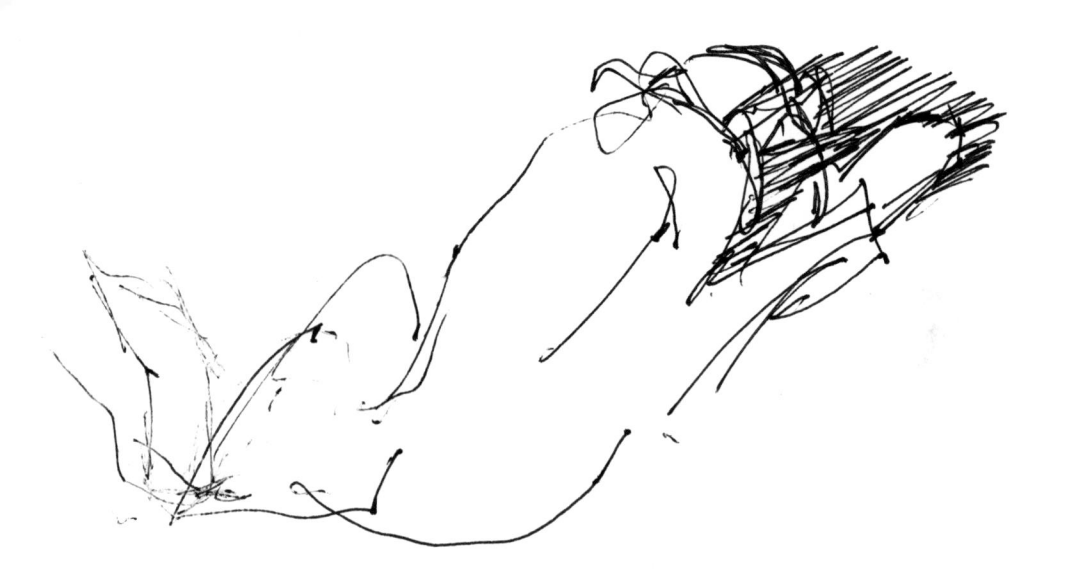

Made in the USA
Lexington, KY
02 March 2017